SUSTAINABLE IMPACT

SUSTAINABLE IMPACT

HOW WOMEN ARE KEY TO ENDING POVERTY

LAINA RAVEENDRAN GREENE
AUDREY TAN
LIZZY HAWKINS

PARTRIDGE

To order additional copies of this book, contact
Toll Free 800 101 2657 (Singapore)
Toll Free 1 800 81 7340 (Malaysia)
orders.singapore@partridgepublishing.com

www.partridgepublishing.com/singapore

CONTENTS

ACKNOWLEDGEMENT

We are truly thankful to God for sending us angels to make this book possible. Indeed we at Angels of Impact strongly believe it is the community of angels shining forth their light that will make a sustainable impact in ending poverty.

The driving force behind Angels of Impact is to find these amazing angels doing great work and create a "cohort of angels" comprising conscious consumers, conscious investors and conscious social entrepreneurs to reinforce each other's efforts. Our goal is to change "business as usual" to "business unusual".

This book was meant as a beacon of light to show that there is already a growing community that can lead the way to end poverty. But to have this book see the light of day has been a truly amazing journey of how many angels come our way to take our vision and make it a reality.

Right from the very beginning when Audrey and I conceived the vision for this book, Lizzy literally appeared from nowhere and had miraculously (given her high-ranking position) the time to pull our ideas and make this book a reality. Once the book was ready, we needed so many more angels to have the book see the light of day.

From editing and proofreading to book design and printing, this has been a very exciting and enriching journey for us. We are passionate about the reasons why we wanted to publish this book and we are simply touched by the hands that came forward to help us in spreading our message to the world.

For starters, our sincere thanks go to Naleeza Ebrahim for stepping up and doing the first edits, which she did over the Christmas and New Year holidays. What a true sacrifice of her time and effort and we most appreciate it. Then came Legha Basiri, who put her meticulous eye for detail to help Naleeza with the second edit of the book. That took many hours of going through the book with a fine-toothed comb, and we know her first trimester of pregnancy definitely did not make it easy either but she still persevered.

However, later Naleeza and Legha were both unable to do the third edit and Lizzy was also busy with her new job. Just as we were about to give up on the book seeing the light of day, we were amazed at how Rita Danani then walked into our lives. Rita had attended a seminar Laina had conducted and she stepped up to volunteer with us. When we realised what her background was, we quickly realised how Godsent she was, as she was key to helping us get this book published. She immediately went to work and opened up her networks to help us complete the last stages of getting the book to the publisher.

She found Faizah Abdul Malik, who runs her own editing firm, Grammar Goondu, and who formerly drafted policies on social enterprises in the Singapore civil service. Faizah did an amazing job editing the book to completion at record speed. Rita also found Faith who helped with referencing, and even Muneera Malik who helped us get our illustrations and diagrams done in parallel. Levonne Goh, Aparna Saxena and Emanuela Longo, all already our angels, collected photos for the book and obtained the requisite permissions to use them.

We would like to thank our spouses Barry Greene, Gerald Tock and Ben Thomas for their moral support and encouragement to make this book a reality. We are so lucky to have husbands who are true HeforShe champions and who support us in our vision to bring together a cohort of angels to help end poverty in this world.

We would like to thank our amazing angel investors Mamoru Taniya, June Tan, Sukanya Pushkarna, Rachel Fitzpatrick, Stephanie Hermawan, Pat Lim, Goh Puay Guan, Keith Chua, Wong Poh Kam, Ronald Walla and Robert Wardhana for investing into our vision, and for the first eight social enterprises for understanding our vision and joining us as members (Toraja Melo, Krakakoa, Javara, Batik Boutique, Siam Organic, Color Silk, The Fabric Social and Mekong Blue). It was their stories that made this book so much richer. Also to Bloomberg Women's Community and Singapore Committee for UN Women for believing in us and helping us with the book launch, and for all those who gave us testimonials, a foreword and introductory remarks for the book. Last but not least, we also want to thank Partridge for being our publisher and for helping us work to get this book out in time for the launch! Their support and encouragement throughout this process were key in moving us forward.

Laina Raveendran Greene & Audrey Tan
Co-founders of Angels of Impact

PRAISE FOR 'SUSTAINABLE IMPACT: HOW WOMEN ARE KEY TO ENDING POVERTY'

"Pithy, pragmatic, heart-warming, shocking—this book tells personal stories of the bottom of the income pyramid. You will learn about social enterprises and how you can and why you should engage. Women are the key to the solution to poverty and this book will convince you of that."

Vint Cerf, Internet Pioneer; "Father of the Internet"; Co-Designer of TCP/IP Protocols; Co-Designer of the architecture of the Internet; Vice-President and Chief Internet Evangelist for Google; and Co-founder and Chairman, People Centered Internet

---

"In the last 100 years, there have been leapfrog developments in technology, transportation and medical facilities. The cliche is that humankind has developed, which is absolutely not true. The progress has benefitted a small percentage of the world's population, leading to increased divisions between rich and poor. The imbalance is leading to increased social unrest in different parts of the world. The existing models of growth and consumption are not sustainable. But what are the other options? The answer lies in the book. It is a guiding force for the next generation of youth who can challenge the status quo and create sustainable models that perpetuate the concept of inclusive development. The book is a breath of fresh air and brings hope that pragmatic solutions are possible in a manner that is socially, financially and environmentally sustainable."

Harish Hande, Co-Founder and Managing Director, SELCO India

"Laina Greene is one of those rare entrepreneurs who has managed to steer their professional career in accordance with their personal values. Her work in stimulating the creation and nurturing of social enterprises is both a sound business initiative and a valuable social service. Her fund enables enterprising women to lift themselves and their partners up from a condition of hopelessness and material poverty, and become active participants in the business community and an inspiration to their peers. This approach has the immense merit of being sustainable, of not requiring bureaucratic government programs of income redistribution, and of empowering disenfranchised populations both materially and spiritually."

Eric Benhamou, Founder and Partner, Benhamou General Ventures

---

"The feminisation of poverty is pervasive and often invisible. The fact that Laina and her friends have formed Angels of Impact to invest in women-led businesses to help women, and are writing about how to do it, makes sense on many levels. Female-led social enterprises, at the early stage, are outperforming their male counterparts by 15% over the first six months of leaving a top-quality accelerator by quantifiable business metrics, yet are 40% less likely to get funding. A network of Angels of Impact nodes springing up to support women-focussed social enterprises would be, to me, brilliant and the highest goal for this book."

Kevin Doyle Jones, Co-founder & Convener, Social Capital Markets; and Founder, Good Capital

---

"Through CRIB (Creating Responsible and Innovative Businesses), a social enterprise empowering women to become successful entrepreneurs, I have met countless women making a positive impact on society and the world. Women have so much to contribute—to their families, the economy and society as a whole. CRIB equips women to reach their full potential, to fulfil their business dream, and leads investors to fund women-led ventures, so we love what Angels of Impact are doing. Equipping women, funding social enterprises and finding solutions to alleviate poverty—their work and this book is exactly what the world needs right now."

Dr Elaine Kim, Co-Founder and CEO, CRIB

"Laina's passion for impact investing is highly infectious and our chapter has definitely benefited from her experience and advice. With Angels of Impact, she is looking to catalyse a favourable ecosystem for women social entrepreneurs—who are not just a good, but a sustainable investment, as well. Her journey in this space and the lessons learnt will be a value-add for anyone who is looking to create an impact in the community by supporting social entrepreneurs."

Sunil Rajan, Co-Chair of Singapore+Acumen (a self-organised volunteer-led chapter of Acumen)

"The book is full of real-life experiences which underscore the importance of practising empathy and humility in order to understand the systemic challenges that perpetuate poverty. The authors have made a compelling argument about how the rising breed of social entrepreneurs in partnership with local communities can turn the tables on inequality and bring about change in millions of families. Reading this book gives us the confidence that it is within our power to turn the utopian vision of a poverty-free world into reality."

Mari Kogiso, Director, Sasakawa Peace Foundation

"Angels of Impact provides great insights that are relevant for audiences all around the world of all generations and backgrounds. At this critical time, having opportunities for impact investors, philanthropists and entrepreneurs to connect, build deep bonds and co-create solutions together is more critical than ever."

**Jenna Nicholas, Managing Partner, Impact Experience;
and President, Phoenix Global Impact**

"The sharing of the real-world journeys, both up and down, in the path to poverty eradication by the authors is interesting. The personal stories are inspiring and show the grit of the authors in pursuing social impact in the face of adversity. The book highlights a salient fact that women are left behind very often, yet opportunities abound to create a world without poverty in unity with women. All the best in your pursuits for women empowerment!"

Eugene Ho, Head of Corporate Affairs, SAP Southeast Asia

"In 2014, the Institute for Healthcare Improvement convened leaders across the world around an audacious goal of 100 million people living healthier lives by 2020. In just 2 years, we have brought together an 'unprecedented collaboration of change agents across sectors' working on mental, physical, social and spiritual wellbeing for all. We are delighted to welcome Angels of Impact into our network of contributors, given their efforts to support women social entrepreneurs alleviating poverty. Overcoming poverty is a key component to social wellbeing, and we are excited to see them have an equally audacious goal of 'creating a world without poverty in unity with women'. This book is timely as it helps change the 'face of poverty' from one of just victims to one of change makers and innovators. It challenges us to see that if we work together we can indeed end poverty for all and unleash the trapped and untapped potential of women around the world to contribute to their wellbeing and the wellbeing of society."

**Dr Somava Stout, Executive Lead, 100M Healthier Lives;
Vice President, Institute for Healthcare Improvement**

"While poverty and women have been greatly talked about, the authors of this book give a distinct account of how women are main actors in addressing not only the economic aspects of poverty, but also its social, cultural, and even political aspects. The authors invite us to embrace with our hearts and minds the notion of feminisation of poverty, and to take actions to end it. This is a must-read book for those looking for the most effective ways of making their lives meaningful in our post-capitalistic society."

Romy Cahyadi, Founder of UnLtd Indonesia

"Through compelling examples of entrepreneurs who are learning how to transform their communities, Laina, Audrey and Lizzy tell the story of a distinctive angel network of 'enterprise philanthropists' who are committed to channelling their resources to find real solutions to poverty. Fellow angel investors have much to learn from their experience."

Dr. Roy Steiner, Senior Director of Learning and Impact, The Omidyar Network

---

"As a development practitioner for the last 20 years working on social development and gender equality, the book by these three women, resonates. I like that the authors shared their experiences of their personal confrontations with issues of poverty and their reflections on how to address poverty through empathy and servitude. Drawing inspirational examples from social entrepreneurs who have empathised and served are remarkable stories of making a difference in people's lives."

Elaine Tan, Executive Director, ASEAN Foundation

"As founding curator of TEDxSingapore, I am inspired to see Audrey and Laina, two Singaporeans from disparate backgrounds and different generations, come together to pursue their common dream of creating a world without poverty in unity with women. In 2016, we invited Angels of Impact to speak at TEDxSingaporeWomen to spread the important idea that 'it is about time to see women as the solution to end poverty'. Their book illustrates how women are leading the way in Asia as change agents."

Dave Lim, Founding Curator of TEDxSingapore

"The book beautifully weaves together stories of social enterprises to depict the ways in which solutions created in partnership with the poor can work toward bringing about transformations. Embodying their own commitments and life experiences, the authors bring together stories that depict the ways in which bottom-up solutions can work within the broader context of poverty. What I find particularly appealing about the many stories of success shared in the book is the overarching ethos of humility and treating the poor with respect and as partners in the creation of solutions that are meaningful to them."

Professor Mohan Dutta
Provost's Chair Professor
Head, Communications and New Media (CNM),
National University of Singapore (NUS)
Director, Center for Culture-Centered Approach
to Research and Evaluation (CARE)
Founder, Center on Poverty and Health Inequities (COPHI)

FOREWORD

I applaud Angels of Impact for exploring the essential topic of feminised poverty, and ways to enable women living in poverty to act as empowered agents of change. By charting their own paths, women from poor backgrounds are also changing the destinies of their families and communities for the better.

Economic empowerment of women is a cause very close to my heart, and also a key component of UN Women's quest to improve the lives of women worldwide. The positive ripple effects also have the potential to change the fabric of societies, even countries and continents, and in simple terms, make the world a better place for everyone. The more human talent included, the better we all do.

The wish to do good in the most efficient way shines through the stories provided by the authors. The Angels of Impact, Laina, Audrey and Lizzy, are sharing their personal journeys across the globe and schools of thought, which led them to the conclusion that social enterprise is the most effective road towards poverty alleviation. The trio walks us through other alternatives to escape poverty, providing an overview easy to grasp for busy practitioners trying to do good, and trying to do it well, while constantly reevaluating how to best do so.

The Angels of Impact provide colourful examples of innovative ventures that shake up existing ways of solving problems of poverty and social ills, attempting to create systemic change with wider impact than the original endeavour. The case stories illustrate that the path might not be straightforward, or easy, but still very much worth it in the end.

The authors tie in three of the UN Sustainable Development Goals (or SDGs) with their efforts, SDG 1: No Poverty, SDG 5: Gender Equality, and SDG 12: Responsible Consumption and Production. The book illustrates that by investing in and consuming responsibly produced goods made by women living in poverty, we advance all three of the global goals at once.

Angels of Impact advocate a network-driven approach to ensure that women, who traditionally have less access to resources, but demonstrate that they as a group use investments wisely, are offered funding and opportunities to build and grow their businesses. The authors are also stressing the importance of locally relevant, empathic approaches rooted in the concept that all of us continue to grow and learn through our stumbles and successes.

I invite readers to enjoy the book, and the captivating arguments for, and accounts of, social enterprises, doing business with the aim of alleviating poverty and creating social good. Read and be inspired by the mosaic of ways forward!

Pia Bruce
Executive Director
Singapore Committee for UN Women

INTRODUCTORY REMARKS

The world has changed rapidly over the past decades. It has become more dynamic than ever, full of unprecedented challenges, and driven by hyper competition. On the other hand, it's becoming more fragile from time to time. As we witness the seemingly unstoppable global warming phenomenon; never-ending poverty; wider gap between the rich and poor; futile and destructive wars; and many other tragedies, we can barely understand why they should happen in the first place. With widespread internet penetration and popularity of social media platforms, the world is truly entering an era of connectivity. Interdependency among countries is inevitable, thus making it even more complex to manage people around the world. That's a snapshot of the world we are living in.

Such formidable challenges perhaps also play a role in fixating the attention of both individuals and companies merely on their own interests and forgetting the unfortunate people out there who desperately need a helping hand. Some of us might be aware of their predicaments and wish to do something but are not quite sure how, where to begin or how to make any such initiative sustainable.

Some companies may also be concerned about these issues, but mostly they are under pressure to focus their attention on achieving strict financial targets. In some cases, the concept of CSR is misused—or perhaps even abused—such that it only functions as a medium to 'compensate a corporate's wrongdoings.' CSR, unfortunately, is sometimes also used to create false perceptions of good corporate citizens. It's a serious dilemma.

Having said that, I believe we are experiencing a severe deprivation of social orientation. I believe all of us agree that we—both as individuals and institutions—should strengthen our social orientation. To do this, we need some practical references that provide guidelines on how to deal with it, particularly poverty issues. This is why I am so delighted that finally three 'superwomen'— Laina, Audrey, and Lizzy—have written and dedicated this great book to all of us.

This is certainly not an ordinary book. It has been constructed based on their firsthand experience in dealing with poverty. Written with passion, it contains more than just knowledge; it is a collection of words of wisdom. It provokes your logic and stretches your heart's horizon.

I met Laina a couple of years back and had a chance to invite her as a speaker to several events in Jakarta. I truly enjoyed her presentations not only because the topics were quite interesting and she delivered them excellently but also, beyond that, they broadened my perspective especially on how to combine two extreme points of a continuum: business and social. Laina's idea is also perfectly aligned with the Marketing 3.0 concept outlined by Hermawan Kartajaya, Founder of MarkPlus, Inc. which talks about why and how a company should shift from products to customers to the human spirit.

What Laina has shared is particularly relevant to me because two years ago, on the 25th anniversary of MarkPlus, Inc., the Council Members decided to publicly declare an initiative of transforming MarkPlus, Inc. to become a social business enterprise. As I read the declaration in front of hundreds of guests, I knew that all of us at MarkPlus, Inc. are fully aware that the institutionalisation of a social aspect is very crucial for the sake of our company's sustainability. We also realise that this won't be easy since we have to renew our vision, recalibrate our mission, and overhaul our values accordingly. We should be able to show the true spirit of humanity based on our existing capabilities and competencies. We should incorporate additional social impact targets on top of various mainstream marketing and financial targets. MarkPlus, Inc. is expected to be fully transformed no later than the year 2020.

It is a daunting task and journey to bravely adopt a social perspective and embed it—not merely as a 'cosmetic attachment'—in your business process and deliver significant impact to all stakeholders. That is why this book is hugely relevant to all of us. Laina, Audrey, and Lizzy have been able to simplify a complex idea about being socially responsible and translate their tacit knowledge into explicit knowledge.

This is not merely a story-telling book that superficially discusses poverty issues and provides you with some great ideas. More than that, this book chronicles the authors' journeys of life, passion, and expression of their calling to make poverty eradication possible.

I am confident that this book will be very useful to us, including the entrepreneurs, to answer difficult questions on how to make an impact on others through actively solving the biggest social ailment that is poverty. Laina, Audrey, and Lizzy are optimistic that poverty can be eradicated if we do something about it. I really like how they have explained the idea of 'feminisation of poverty' so we can better understand why poverty has a greater impact on women than men. Interestingly, women are usually the victims, but at the same time, they are also the most important element to solve poverty.

Laina, Audrey, and Lizzy believe that poverty is rooted in so many other causes and if you are really concerned about this, then sympathy plus 'band-aids' are no longer enough, that's not a recipe for change. There should be a strong sense of caring, humility, and empathy followed by real action.

Negative thinking and sceptical attitudes towards the poor always prevent us from embracing them, and in turn makes them silent victims, not partners. The authors also explain some challenges in order to make impactful charity and donations, though there are limitations to that approach. That is why they suggest to us to go beyond charity—through social enterprises where better businesses can indeed make a better world.

Laina, Audrey, and Lizzy also point out that though social enterprises are ideal, we have to be mindful of several challenges that might obstruct our good intentions. They also share important insights on why some social enterprises are struggling. In the end, they remind us that everything is back again to you: how you live your life driven by purpose, how you, as an individual, can truly make a difference and influence others to do the same.

This is the right book for the optimists, and for the sceptics. Don't worry, just read it and you will be transformed.

I would like to congratulate Laina, Audrey, and Lizzy. I wish you and your Angels of Impact can truly create a world without poverty in unity with women.

Dr Jacky Mussry
Deputy CEO
MarkPlus, Inc.

INTRODUCTION

Here are some reasons for you to read this book:

> *You donate to charity, but wonder if your money is really making an impact.*

> *You are curious about social entrepreneurship, and how it can solve issues underlying poverty in a more sustainable way.*

> *You are sceptical but intrigued with the notion that poverty can be eradicated if we were all to do something about it.*

> *Perhaps you have never wondered why when asked to think of an image of a poor person, more often than not, you think of a woman with a child begging by the side of the road.*

Through reading this book, you will learn more about the 'feminisation of poverty' and understand how women are the main victims of this social ailment. You will also learn that we can in fact end poverty—with data pointing to women as the key agents to eradicating it.[1]

'We'—Laina, Audrey and Lizzy—wrote this book together. We are three women from very different walks of life who share a passion for poverty eradication. We have separately spent our lives looking for effective and fulfilling means to help end poverty in positive ways and have arrived at the same conclusion. Whether in the field of charity, law, government, or business, we all saw clearly that women are in fact the key agents to end poverty; unfortunately, their attempts all over the world are hampered by their lack of access to the resources required to achieve widespread impact.

Since life serendipitously brought us together, we decided to start Angels of Impact to help support and champion social enterprises working to 'create a world without poverty in unity with women'. We are energised, inspired and enthused by our realisation that channelling resources and opportunities to **social enterprises can offer better solutions** to global problems, such as poverty, than those offered by traditional charities, profit-first businesses or even governments.

We will fire your imagination with the achievements of some amazing social enterprises working to help end poverty. You will learn how their brilliant solutions have had enormous and enriching effects—far beyond what is commonly achieved in the pursuit of profit-maximisation-driven businesses, traditional charity or government aid.

Finally, we will demonstrate simple ways for you to actively support social enterprises so that they can increase their impact.

First, let us go back to the beginning and tell you about ourselves, so you know where we come from and how we have arrived here.

OUR PERSONAL JOURNEYS

Laina Raveendran Greene

I was born in Singapore in the 1960s to parents who had emigrated from India in search of a better future. Through sheer hard work and sacrifice, they were able to offer my sisters and me opportunities for a much-improved life. Throughout my childhood, my parents insisted that we did social work for the less fortunate in Singapore. It taught us to be grateful for what we had.

This was important, as we were often surrounded by people who had more than we did. Having been raised to live a life of service, I was drawn to work for the UN in Geneva in the hope of serving humanity better. So I persuaded my parents to send me for graduate studies in Geneva. It was quite a sacrifice for them, but they somehow made it work. It was during my time in Geneva that I began to explore business models that could do good socially while doing well financially—what we know today as 'social enterprise'.

While serving as an intern in Geneva at International Telecommunications Union (ITU) in 1986, and later as a working professional at International Satellite Organization (INTELSAT) in Washington DC, I worked in social ventures on a global scale. I helped ensure that member countries could provide affordable communication service in rural areas, so that they would not be left behind by the rising information economy.[2] At that time, the telecommunications industry was moving from being run by governments to being run by private entities. There was great concern that private entities may not want to provide telecommunication services to rural areas, where profit margins were small to non-existent. I was determined to make the case that you can do good—provide connectivity for all, and bridge the digital divide—and still do well financially.

The concept of 'social enterprise' did not exist in those days, yet I was already searching for business models to bridge the digital divide. Even 'Corporate Social Responsibility' (CSR) was not a term that was on the radar. Government intervention was still required to either regulate, or mandate, private companies to mitigate the digital divide, as there was little or no business case to extend telecommunications in rural areas. In some instances, governments set up funds into which telecoms companies paid taxes or fees when they renewed their licences. These funds were then used to subsidise the cost of bridging the digital divide.

But I quickly realised that all these regulations and efforts to cross-subsidise telecoms services still did not end the digital divide. There was more to it than just technology or money.

I noticed that the digital divide was closely tied to the energy divide. Without energy, telecommunications was useless. Just as I realised it was not simply money or technology that would solve the problem of the digital divide, I also began to see that we needed innovative business models such as grassroots social enterprises bridging the energy and digital divide.

I learnt how Grameen Phone used local women as telephone ladies to bring telecommunications to rural areas. In later years, as the cost of technology dropped and regulations were not as restrictive, I saw grassroots entrepreneurs make it profitable to deliver energy at the 'last mile'. Grameen Shakti and SELCO—companies that bring renewable energy to low-income communities using new financing tools—taught me that the right technology and innovative business models can help grassroots social enterprises to dramatically reduce the cost of doing business and make rural service-providers profitable.

In 1997, I started my own business to bring e-learning to developing countries. We were such pioneers in those days that CNN and Channel News Asia covered our work. We used a cross-subsidisation model by working with high-paying corporations like Cisco to help subsidise e-learning services to Laos, Vietnam, Cambodia and Thailand. In many ways, we were actually functioning as a social enterprise—though we did not yet know that term—as our primary social goal was to work on equal access to information and learning for all.

In later years, I saw the growth of other tech social entrepreneurs. Air Jaldi, for example, was offering broadband Internet services in the remotest mountain villages of Dharamsala, India, and making money! It was more profitable for a social enterprise with local context and connections to offer services than for a big urban company to do so. The cost of rolling out infrastructure, acquiring and then maintaining customers was just too high for the urban big boys.

I finally came across the term 'social enterprise', and learnt about innovative social enterprise models while guest lecturing at Stanford in 2007 and judging the Stanford BASES Social Challenge.[3] In the following years, I became very involved in social enterprise work in the United States and Europe.

In 2008, I came across Professor Muhammad Yunus' book, 'Creating a World Without Poverty', and it struck at the core of my being. He challenges us all to do something about eradicating poverty by 2030, and put poverty into museums. He introduced a new model of social enterprise called 'social business' (more about this on pages xxxix).

By then, I had sold my e-learning company and was looking for my next endeavour. Having been inspired by the stories of SELCO, Grameen Shakti and Air Jaldi, among others, I wanted to start a fund to help replicate successful social enterprise models around the region. I managed to raise money from the World Wildlife Fund (WWF) in Sweden, and together with SELCO Founder, Harish Hande and others, we conducted a gap analysis to see what the fund should do. There were many great suggestions. However, the 2008 global financial crisis stopped us in our tracks.

I wanted to have the fund focus on women, as I was very aware of the unconscious biases that lead to women having less access to funding than men. For example, in Silicon Valley, where I lived and worked for over 16 years, the Wall Street Journal reported in 2016 that a mere 7% of venture funding reaches women founders. Having been a female techpreneur in Singapore and Silicon Valley, even before technopreneurship was popular, I had first-hand experience of how hard it was to be a woman entrepreneur.

Putting my dream of the fund on hold during the financial crisis, I worked for an internet social enterprise making domain names software accessible to anyone who needed it. A year and a half later, I received an offer to run an Innovation Investment fund for a conglomerate in Indonesia. While meeting the billionaire owner of that company in his Beverly Hills mansion, I told him about my desire to start a fund for women social entrepreneurs. He was intrigued and suggested that I work with him first and create that fund later, possibly with his support. Knowing that Indonesia has a population of 255 million people, with 11.2% living below the poverty line,[4] I felt I could do more there than in Singapore or Silicon Valley. I grabbed the opportunity.

In Indonesia, however, I was immediately reassigned to a sister company of the conglomerate, a telecom tower company. I focussed mainly on fundraising but had the opportunity to introduce some aspects of CSR around 'green' information communication technology (ICT). To fulfil my passion for poverty alleviation, I extended my personal network and initiated projects to help women. I started by funding scholarships for my driver's children and helping my maid create her own business to be closer to her village. All this felt good, but the impact was small. Through the local Rotary Club, a friend and I helped co-fund an NGO for 20,000 women to make crafts from home and earn money. Again, it felt good, but the impact was not sustainable as the project lacked a business model and therefore required constant fresh funds for its survival.

Upon a friend's recommendation, UnLtd Indonesia, an organisation nurturing aspiring social entrepreneurs, sought me out as their advisor when they were setting up in Jakarta. Helping UnLtd Indonesia fund and mentor social enterprises were extremely rewarding and impactful for me. It convinced me that social enterprise was the more scalable and sustainable way to make a difference. Through UnLtd Indonesia, I met Dinny Jusuf, the founder of Toraja Melo, a social enterprise creating fashion and gift items from hand-woven textiles produced by indigenous women weavers and put together by skilled poor women in towns. She truly inspired me. She proved right my theory that women-led social enterprises are the key agents in poverty alleviation. I met many more persevering women who had made great strides in alleviating poverty, such as Tri Mumpuni, founder of IBEKA, which partners with rural communities to produce hydroelectricity; and Helianti Hillman, founder of Javara, a social enterprise working with smallholder farmers across Indonesia to retail artisanal food products, just to name a couple.

At the close of my two-year contract, my boss no longer seemed keen on the fund I had previously proposed. To remain in Indonesia, I agreed to be Senior Advisor of Ashoka, a network for social entrepreneurs. Through Ashoka, I met more social entrepreneurs. Ashoka opened my eyes to another element of successful social enterprise: the concept of systems change. A true social entrepreneur does not just do good, but makes lasting change through altering systems that are ineffective. Ashoka also taught me the importance of empathy and passion for successful entrepreneurship. Empathy requires context, and people who live where the problems lie have greater empathy and context and are more likely to devise better solutions—key components of human-centric design. Additionally, someone who has had a defining moment, which makes them passionate about solving a problem, is more likely to persevere until reaching success than one without a similar experience.

After all these experiences and learning, serendipity reunited me in Indonesia with a former student from my guest-lecturing days at Stanford. I had taught Audrey Tan and mentored her venture, PlayMoolah, at its inception. She had already become a successful social entrepreneur in Singapore and the region. Audrey convinced me to return to Singapore. She was intrigued by my idea of a fund to help, mentor and open doors for women social entrepreneurs, so we decided to join forces. Shortly after that, Lizzy Hawkins—a friend from Jakarta—moved to Singapore and called to ask if I was doing anything interesting. She decided to join us. Together we managed to get 11 other entrepreneur friends to invest in our vision of creating Angels of Impact.

And the rest is history!

Audrey Tan

'Others before self' was a practice inculcated by my parents, especially my mother. I was told to share candies and biscuits with others before eating any. I used to be really upset with my mother for that, but I have since learnt that generosity goes a long way. Like the parable of the woman with only two pennies, who gave from her lack all that she had, not from her excess; I witnessed my parents supporting charities and giving selflessly in church every Sunday, even though they were not well off. It showed me that you can always help others, no matter how little you have. I began to understand through their generosity that we do not have to be millionaires to donate and do good work; we always have something to give.

I was lucky to have access to practical experience with computers at a young age. In 2005, I started my first e-commerce blog. I was 18 and in my first year at university. It was a very simple trading model to bring women's clothes to the market, as technology allowed you to easily access the world. My second e-commerce blog leveraged on bulk buying, similar to the Groupon[5] model for clothing. Hundreds of women bought from me. That was my income at age 18.

Access to a university education also meant that I had exposure to programmes that would shape my perspective of the world. In 2008, I was incredibly fortunate to have been one of five women, out of 27 applicants, selected for the National University of Singapore's (NUS) Overseas College (NOC) programme. I applied to work and study in Silicon Valley. It was incredibly humbling to work alongside the best innovators and have the privilege to study in Stanford. I met Laina there and she became our mentor at PlayMoolah in the early days. I am deeply grateful for my education, knowing that a different reality exists for other women around the world. A United Nations Educational, Scientific and Cultural Organization (UNESCO) report on literacy rates stated that women are less likely to get a secondary education than men.[6] Globally, 62 million girls miss out on school and make up two-thirds of the world's illiterate population.[7] To be honest, there are days when I wake up and find myself asking, "What did I do to deserve all these opportunities?"

As part of my NOC module in the Valley, I joined Qik.com, which was at the cutting-edge of technology. Qik pioneered streaming live videos from mobile phones, similar to what we now know as Apple's FaceTime. The founders—Bhaskar Roy, Nickolay Abkairov, Vijay Tellar and Ramu Sunkara—had a vision and found ways to execute it. I was exhilarated to be among pioneers who found ways and means to disrupt the status quo, bringing technology that would drive new behaviours in users.

Qik's founders were disruptors and showed me that if you identify a need in the market, and have the restlessness and intuition to act on it, your solution could really change the world. Qik was eventually preloaded on all non-Apple devices around the world[8] and Skype acquired it for US$150M in 2011.[9] It taught me to just DO! There is a mantra, 'Do 99%, think 1%'. I try to practice it.

I was in the Bay Area in the midst of the 2008 global financial crisis. Along with Min, my roommate, I investigated the root causes of poor money decisions in households across America. Our hypothesis was simple: if we could imbue good money habits in children at a young age, they might take those habits into adulthood. As we spoke to many American families, we realised that parents were struggling to manage their own finances. Parents themselves often did not know the best practices when it came to money.

Min and I founded PlayMoolah while still in the U.S., using play, digital tools and community experiences to inspire children to save, earn, give, spend and invest. We worked with financial institutions, schools, organisations and parents to foster money conversations and enable children to make informed financial decisions and have greater financial resilience. We then created WhyMoolah, a decision-making tool for young adults, now being used by over 60,000 people worldwide. As we explored how to enable people to manage money better, we gained deeper insights into relationships to money and explored new definitions of wealth within a framework formulated by permaculture experts Ethan Roland & Gregory Landua[10].

Having impacted over 100,000 people with PlayMoolah, I hungered to do more, especially once I returned to Asia. My first visit to Jakarta in 2013 planted the seed for the growth of Angels of Impact. I met Lynna Chandra, who was running a hospice for dying, impoverished children who could not afford mainstream healthcare. There, on the streets, a young child with a baby on her back tapped on our car window to ask for money. I was shocked at the sight; this was the first time abject poverty knocked on my door. Lynna told me about the slum children who begged in order to live. I shared with her my desire to do more work with the poor and she informed me about Sekolah Bisa, a slum school in south Jakarta. She suggested sharing some of my lessons from PlayMoolah with the children. I had never thought of giving my time to charity! I realised that the barrier to serving was so much lower than I had thought, and that I did not have to wait till I was a millionaire.

I began to understand the importance of listening to needs within a community, rather than imposing ideas on what should be fixed. I had *an enlightening experience through meeting Wiwid, a teacher at Sekolah Bisa at the time. She had been a domestic helper in Singapore and Jakarta. The teaching job was a step up for her. When I asked Wiwid during one conversation what her dream was, she revealed that she wanted to become a special needs teacher, but the fees were too high at S$3,000. I started an Indiegogo campaign with a few friends from PlayMoolah and raised the money in three weeks. Listening to Wiwid had helped me understand her aspirations, which then opened a path to greater social mobility and growth for her. It was incredibly humbling, and pivotal, in making me realise that the wealth in the world simply needs proper stewardship towards relevant needs.*

With the immense opportunities and resources at my disposal, could I change the lives of ten more Wiwids, or a hundred?

I had been on mission trips to Thailand and parts of Kenya, where we simply trekked to remote villages, delivered supplies, congratulated ourselves and then left. We did not realise that the models of charity and donations were not always sustainable. However, after a visit to Toraja, Indonesia, I saw how social enterprises like Toraja Melo can truly impact and change many lives. I was stunned by the magnitude of work done by Dinny, the founder of Toraja Melo; she was changing lives in entire villages. A consistent supply of the village women's handiwork to the wider economic market gave them steady incomes; it was an alternative career to being a domestic helper or a sex worker.

A quote from the gospel of Matthew 13:12 says, "To anyone that has, more will be given. And to the one that has not, even what he seems to have will be taken away." I stretch it to mean, "You have been given so much in terms of responsibility, time, money, talent or knowledge; these have been entrusted to you and ought to be given away generously."

Poverty poses such a pressing challenge in today's world that it demands a collective response to systematically and effectively harness resources and wealth to alleviate it. It was this thought process that eventually led me towards the inception of Angels of Impact.

Lizzy Hawkins

It has always been more important to me to make a difference than to make money. My whole working life felt like training to build the requisite skills needed to change the world. As I grew older, I began to despair that I might never reach the point where I would be so able. I realised that I had to start with what I had and who I was, however imperfect!

I had been donating regularly to charities for issues that I cared about. After graduating from university, I moved to London and wanted to do more. I started volunteering with a charity for the homeless. At first, I was happy to see our guests relaxing in a safe space and basked in their gratitude. It felt good that I was giving my time to make it possible. But the same people came back, year after year. Their problems with addiction, mental health, criminal convictions, lack of education and lack of any money to invest in their futures meant they were stuck in a vicious cycle.

There were glimmers of bright spots. Of the hundreds—maybe thousands—someone, somehow was able to transform their lives. One man, Malcolm, obtained a grant to qualify as a lorry driver and got a job and then a place to live. One woman, Yolanta, after years of completely debilitating alcoholism, found the courage to seek treatment. The next time I saw her, she was almost unrecognisable—and volunteering alongside me for the same charity. But successes like these were a handful among hundreds. It was frustrating to see all the hard work doing so little to really transform lives.

I continued to chase a profession where I could change the world. I joined the government sector because I thought it was the best place from which to make far-reaching changes. In retrospect, I was naïve. In the British Civil Service, the Minister makes the decisions and our job is to make sure that he/she gets the best possible, best-researched options, and his/her decision is delivered to the best possible standards. It is fascinating work, but not the way for an individual to change things.

So I remained on the lookout for ways of changing the world which did not involve constant begging for money, or being a small cog in a big machine.

I realised long ago that most people—myself included, a lot of the time—like the idea of doing good, but only if it does not inconvenience them. So the idea of making it easy and attractive to do good was a compelling proposition. One way to do that is through having social enterprises focus on providing high-quality goods or services, so people do not have that sinking feeling, "Oh, I suppose I should buy this for charity—even though it's rubbish." People should be able to say, "Why thank you! I'd love to buy it. This is a great bag," and then think, "When I buy it, I can help to ensure that a whole family in remote Indonesia is educated, well-fed and healthy."

Social enterprises amaze me; the ingenuity and courage of people who come up with an idea that makes money and helps transform people's lives is inspiring. Since learning about social enterprise, I have researched about it—including reading Professor Muhammad Yunus' book, 'A World Without Poverty', which I loved because of his unequivocal, practical vision of what a world without poverty should look like.

Then I met Laina at a party at the British Deputy Ambassador's house in Jakarta. When she said, "My real passion is social enterprise," I yelped, "Ooh, tell me more!" But my life in Jakarta was too hectic for me to do anything substantial with Laina and social enterprise at the time. Then I fell ill and left Jakarta. (On a side note—heed your doctor's warnings about avoiding deep-vein-thrombosis on long flights! Pulmonary emboli are not fun.) Upon recovery, I joined my fiancé in Singapore to be a lady of leisure. Knowing Laina had moved to Singapore too, I contacted her and asked if there was any social enterprise I could help with. There was. This is it!

I am so thrilled to have had the opportunity to work with Laina and Audrey in creating Angels of Impact.

ABOUT ANGELS OF IMPACT

Our inspiration for starting Angels of Impact came from reading Professor Muhammad Yunus' book, *Creating a World without Poverty*. We were very moved by his thesis that poverty can be eliminated and showcased in museums as a thing of the past, if we all did something about it. We were also very moved by his thesis that charity robs the poor of dignity. He compares the poor to bonsai trees, explaining that the only difference between them and a great big tree is that they have little access to the resources and opportunities needed in order to flourish. The poor have innovative ideas and the capability to take themselves out of poverty, if given a chance, and provided with adequate and appropriate support.

Meanwhile, the three of us were also shocked to find that despite all the international development efforts to help people get out of poverty, women are usually left behind. Given that women are subjugated in many societies, they are the ones left to walk for miles to collect firewood and water, take care of the young and old, carry out subsistence farming and weave, or take part in other crafts in the evenings to provide additional income for the families. Therefore, they are usually not offered the opportunity to take advantage of efforts to alleviate poverty. Professor Muhammad Yunus was one of the first to publicly recognise women as good investments. It was thus a no-brainer for us to have Angels of Impact focus on eradicating the feminisation of poverty and promote women as key agents of change.

Professor Muhammad Yunus moved from only funding micro-businesses to also funding social businesses (more about this on pages xxxix). That made us realise that women-led micro-businesses in turn need help accessing markets and funding. We came across some inspiring social enterprises trying to meet this need; however, they too were struggling. We thought we would be able to make a greater impact if we helped a social entrepreneur like Dinny Jusuf, the founder of Toraja Melo, who in turn helps over 1,000 women weavers, rather than trying to help one woman micro-entrepreneur at a time. We realised that even in developed countries, educated women entrepreneurs often have difficulty raising funds; no wonder then that this is so problematic for women entrepreneurs in developing nations. With a focus on poverty alleviation, this task becomes even more difficult. The Monitor Group report, *From Blueprint to Scale*[11], shows that most impact investors do not like to focus on poverty. We therefore decided to focus on women-led social enterprises tackling poverty.

The massive transformative purpose of Angels of Impact is 'creating a world without poverty in unity with women'. We support women-led social enterprises helping to alleviate poverty, hand in hand with men. By creating an ecosystem, in which resources can flow to where they are needed most, we can ensure the sustainability and success of these social enterprises.

The thinking behind Angels of Impact is to enable everyone, not just the wealthy, to use their money and capital in a more conscious and responsible way, and also to shop consciously. Oxfam has a sobering projection that since 2015, the richest 1% of the world has owned more wealth than the rest of the planet.[12] That leaves 99% of the world sharing 1% of the wealth. How, and why, did this happen and how can we steward money to flow to places of need instead?

We noticed that a lot of networks channelling money to charity, or impact investing, often cross-invest in each other's funds, and these funds are usually not accessible to ordinary people. Membership costs a lot of money and you have to be an accredited investor or originate from a family foundation. Angels of Impact hopes to bring about change through a more inclusive model, by enabling more people to channel their money into support for social enterprises. Through promoting and selling goods on behalf of social enterprises, we aim to inspire people to become conscious consumers.

Angels of Impact passionately believes that together, we can achieve at least three of the seventeen United Nations Sustainable Development Goals: Goal #1: No Poverty, Goal #5: Gender Equality, and Goal #12: Responsible Consumption and Production.

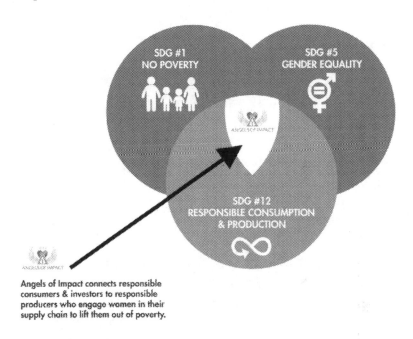

Angels of Impact connects responsible consumers & investors to responsible producers who engage women in their supply chain to lift them out of poverty.

Figure 1. Diagram showing how Angels of Impact's work addresses three of the UN SDG goals.

To learn more about Angels of Impact, please visit www.angelsofimpact.com.

What we do is 1) enable people to channel their money into support for social enterprises, and 2) promote and sells goods on behalf of social enterprises, to engender conscious consumers. By investing in, and consuming, responsibly-produced goods made by women living in poverty, you achieve all three goals at once.

We wrote this book to help create a movement of conscious investors and consumers.

How to use this book

We will begin with definitions, which will help to put some things into perspective.

Some Definitions

Being familiar with the terms and their definitions below would be helpful as you read this book. We have also included a glossary at the end of the book for your convenience.

People tend to use the terms *social entrepreneur*, *social enterprise*, and *social business* interchangeably, but these terms actually refer to different things.

A **social entrepreneur** is someone who designs an innovative solution to a social problem. But not all social entrepreneurs set up social enterprises. A social entrepreneur might merely campaign for a change in the law to solve a social problem. He or she might believe that a social enterprise model is not the right solution to a problem and decide to set up a non-profit organisation instead. So while many social entrepreneurs set up social enterprises, not all of them do. Ashoka, the pioneer organisation that coined the term 'social entrepreneur' in the 1970s, has some key criteria that distinguish a person as a social entrepreneur. To be an Ashoka fellow, you must have a new idea that has the potential to cause systems-change, demonstrate creativity and entrepreneurship, and you must be a person of integrity.[13]

A **social enterprise** is a business that prioritises impact over profit. It aims to make profit so it can expand its impact, but ultimately impact is the most important thing. The amount of profit expectations will vary, depending on the type of investors involved and the sectors they operate in. Social enterprises may also be known as businesses driven by purpose before profit or purpose-driven businesses, and social impact before profit businesses. Their purpose could be poverty alleviation, or increasing access to education, or reducing the impact to the environment, but they all fundamentally strive to solve social problems using business fundamentals.[14]

A **social business** is a type of social enterprise, but focusses primarily on addressing the needs of the poor. The term was popularised by Professor Muhammad Yunus, founder of Grameen Bank. He has seven criteria he uses to define a social business. These are: 1) a social business' obejctives will be to overcome poverty, or one or more problems (such as education, health, technology access, and environment) which threaten people and society; not profit-maximisation, 2) financial and economic sustainability, 3) investors get back their investment amount only. No dividend is given beyond investment money, 4) when investment amount is paid back, company profit stays with the company for expansion and improvement, 5) the social business is gender sensitive and environmentally conscious, 6) the workforce gets market wage with better working conditions, and 7) the social business does it with joy.[15] Professor Muhammad Yunus has established several social businesses such as Grameen Bank, Grameen Shakti, Grameen Phone, and many more with well-known multinational companies. Grameen Danone provides fortified yoghurt to poor communities in Bangladesh; Grameen Veolia brings clean drinking water to Bangladeshi villages; and Grameen Adidas aims to ensure that no one goes without shoes. As these examples show, social businesses can involve partnerships with big companies who usually come in with money and technology.

Micro businesses are fundamentally smaller than small and medium enterprises. They are typically businesses selling vegetables, cooked food, groceries or other items. They are also usually run by people who have no other options, sometimes also known as "entrepreneurs by necessity".

Next, we examine some business practices that can easily be confused with social enterprises. Businesses that carry out the following practices seek to do social and/or environmental good, but are not considered social enterprises. They are better known as socially responsible companies.

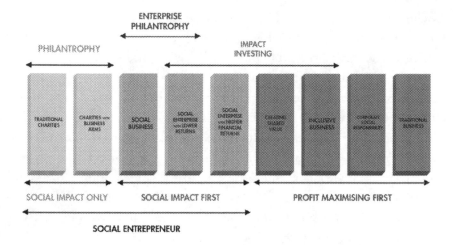

SPECTRUM OF BUSINESS AND INVESTING MODELS

Figure 2

Corporate Social Responsibility (CSR) is where businesses try to reduce the harm that they do to the world while enhancing their positive impacts. Some might try to reduce their environmental consequences and publicise the progress of their efforts, or even become carbon-neutral. Others might provide free goods and/or services to local schools or community groups. Several might sponsor charities or encourage employees to volunteer for good causes.[16]

CSR enables companies to build goodwill in the communities they operate in. It has become normal for companies— particularly high-profile ones—to adopt responsible business practices.[17] Some do this out of genuine commitment to responsible business; others do it because they know they are being scrutinised by vocal consumer groups; and many others do it to keep up with their competitors.

CSR is an add-on to the main, profit-first business. CSR is about responsible business—but only as far as it does not hurt the bottom line.[18]

Inclusive business is another term you will hear about, coined by the World Business Council for Sustainable Development (WBCSD) in 2005.[19] Inclusive businesses are companies that aim to include the world's marginalised people into their business structures and processes, either as customers, employees or suppliers. The difference between a social enterprise and an inclusive business is their primary focus. Social enterprises are focussed on making social impact by trying to improve people's lives. They solve problems through ways that make money, in order to be self-sufficient and continue growing. On the other hand, inclusive businesses are focussed on profit first and then try to fit poorer communities into their business model in an attempt to do social good and/or be seen as good corporate citizens.

There is another fairly new approach called **Creating Shared Value (CSV)**, introduced in 2011 by Professor Michael Porter from Harvard Business School.[20] This approach embraces social good as part of a company's core business strategies; the products they create inherently do good as they have clear economic, societal and/or environmental benefits and does resemble social enterprises but it is not. It does this through:

- Re-conceiving products and markets in ways that meet customer needs while also contributing to society;
- Redefining productivity in the company's value chain through social or environmental innovations; and/or
- Cluster development—this involves companies supporting the wellbeing of industries related to their business in ways that improve overall societal conditions. For example, they can begin to procure goods and services from related social enterprises in a more sustainable way.

At the other end of the spectrum are the **business arms of charities**. For example, they may offer paid-for consultancy or sell greetings cards and gifts for profit, which they then channel to the charity. If that brings in more money for them to do their work, it is good news. But they are not social enterprises because they are still largely donation-dependent. The income they make from these business activities is usually small and just supplements their funds from donations.

Impact investors aim to achieve positive social impact while still making money from their investments. Some impact investors ensure that the companies in which they invest meet certain social and environmental standards; others focus on particular sectors and invest in companies that have high potential to make big changes. So an impact investor might focus on healthcare and invest in a new model of health insurance or a medical technology company that will improve healthcare while making money. Not all impact investors invest purely in social enterprises. Like all the terms we have defined, this is great too; impact investing helps promising companies to grow and spurs the rest of the business community to improve their practices.

All of these approaches—CSR, inclusive businesses, CSV, and charities selling products or services—are good ideas moving in the right direction. However, social enterprise (including social business) is the one approach that shows the most promise in ending poverty, given the high cost of doing business. It does not treat people as cold, economic units like traditional businesses do and yet works to ensure sustainability. It is revolutionary and we need to support these efforts so they can survive and grow.

A brief look at the chapters of this book

Chapters 1 and 2 look at the big picture—global poverty. We will explain that global poverty is an ill that can be eradicated, and ending it makes an enormous impact on many other issues that you care about.

You may say that poverty is not the issue that concerns you the most, but we will show you how poverty is at the root of the very issues that matter to you. Poverty can be linked to people dying of diseases, to social ills like corruption, slavery, migration, abuse of women, and even to deforestation. You will discover the shocking truth that poor people are often paying much more for the exact same things that we take for granted—in absolute terms, not just proportionally.

We will show you how there is hope, in the form of women. Discover why women are the most powerful players in the mission to end poverty. You will find evidence that women's actions make a huge difference to a family's wellbeing. We share how women have, again and again, proven to be good investments in business and daily life.

Chapter 3 reveals how humility and empathy have to be your most important characteristics when acting on the issues that you care about. When you propose to solve a problem with humility and *ask* how you can serve, you will be far more effective than if you assume you have the solutions; you will design human-centric solutions, which are better and sustainable.

We will bust myths and assumptions about the poor and needy being lazy, ignorant, uncaring, and reveal successful innovations that have come straight from the poorest places in the world. Amazing things have emerged in partnership with the impoverished. Invariably, efforts have failed when people have taken a patronising approach and proposed solutions without respecting the reality of life on the ground.

Chapter 4 discusses charity and donations. If you are reading this book, you are probably already giving to charity, and feel as though you need to give more and more while doubting if you are having any impact at all. We will get to the root of why that is so frustrating, and explain why a model based on donations actually restricts charities and non-profit groups from growing.

Chapter 5 takes the theme of humility and empathy a step further by looking at the need to initiate systems change. You should start asking why the existing systems have failed from the beneficiaries' perspective rather than merely formulating solutions for the problems caused by those systemic failures. A 'systems-change' approach can lead to lasting impact, especially when viewed through the lens of humility and empathy.

Chapter 6 delves deep into purpose-driven social enterprises. Learn how they are pioneering responsible capitalism, which focusses on social impact before profit. Meet some of the social enterprises we support and discover their positive alternatives to profit-maximising businesses. We will show how 'social enterprises' especially those run by women are making a real impact in ending poverty.

Chapter 7 explains why social enterprises have it harder than profit-maximising businesses and how that has led to a 'pioneer gap' for social enterprises struggling to get the support they need to grow.

Finally, the **Conclusion** unveils how you can live a more conscious, joyful and authentic life. See what you can do to support a world of purpose-driven businesses. We will give you the opportunity to join us in building a new type of capitalism, where people and purpose are more important than just focussing on profit.

We all know that is how the world should be, and now we offer you a way to support and be part of that world. It does not matter how much money you have, or what job you do; YOU can help make a better world today. There is no need even to quit your job to join an NGO to truly make a difference. So what can you do to end poverty?

CHAPTER 1

BANISH POVERTY

*"When you're fighting extreme poverty, optimism is a moral choice.
Pessimism in the face of extreme poverty can become a self-fulfilling
prophecy that is deadly for the poor."*
– Jim Yong Kim, World Bank Group President[21]

Global poverty is huge. Nearly half of the world's population—2.8 billion people—survives on less than US$2 a day.[22] But even those who have escaped poverty are constantly at risk of slipping back.

It is easy for an individual looking at those numbers to feel helpless and wonder if one could ever make a meaningful dent in those huge numbers.

Do not be discouraged. But do be humble and start with small deeds. Humility is important to help us understand the reality of the problems so we can find the best solutions. It helps us understand that our impact will always be small in the grand scheme of things; yet, we must not hesitate to act—because if we do not act, we will have no impact at all. Small acts can cause ripple effects for huge impact.

What does poverty mean to you? Do you even know what life is like for the poor?

"In 2013, it really shook my world to see children begging in Indonesia and to learn that their parents had sent them there. Fast-forward to 2016, Anshu Gupta, founder of the Indian social movement Goonj, asked me, 'Do you think the parents really wanted to do that?' And I realised they really did not have a choice. So at the time I had just a simplistic understanding, 'What awful parents!' I was using my own Singaporean lens to judge. But the reality is that they were living in slums, surrounded by trash—mostly plastic—that they had to burn to dispose of. From a health standpoint, that was terrible. As you go through the villages, you see that there is no proper water and sanitation; trash right outside their homes; no bathrooms, toilets and shower facilities; and the children are walking barefoot. You then quickly realised that they had no other options." – Audrey Tan

When you have never experienced poverty, you do not realise how dreadful it can be. You do not realise that when you are poor, you do not just lack money. That much is obvious. But poverty is a darker place than that; it means hunger, lack of education, poor health and shorter life expectancy. Imagine having to choose between using fuel to cook food for your children or to boil water to make it safe for them to drink. Imagine choosing between borrowing from a dangerous loan shark whom you probably cannot pay back or not being able to buy vital medicine for your mother. Imagine choosing between marrying your 13 year-old daughter off to a nearby family, even though you know she would essentially become their slave, or watching her starve because the rains did not come and your harvest is lost.

Poverty is about having no good options.

"I grew up in a nice house in a small village. It was a comfortable upbringing and I only knew about poverty from books and TV. I had a vague notion of poor people as being sad and beaten-down, either frightening criminals or good-hearted and humble. I know, it was a deeply patronising attitude, which I'm still trying to shake off. Working with the guests at the shelters I volunteered at helped to change this.

"It took me a long time to understand that these guests were hardly responsible for their poverty and homelessness. Every decision that had led them to that point had been reasonable at the time—leaving home to escape abuse; moving to the other end of the country to live with the man

she loved, who became her abuser; borrowing money to start a company; sofa-surfing with friends after leaving his wife, until it got too much to ask to stay again; getting drunk to escape the cold and the reality of where he'd ended up. People who had recently become homeless were usually shocked and silent. They didn't understand how they'd ended up in this place, even though when they looked back, the story was so clear." – Lizzy Hawkins

Being poor is expensive: the 'Bottom of the Pyramid' Penalty

We must discuss another aspect of poverty that often keeps people in this vicious cycle. Did you know that life is actually more expensive for the very poor than it is for people with a bit more money? This is called the 'Bottom of the Pyramid Penalty' (BOP Penalty). Life for the very poor is very costly, not just because things are more expensive as a proportion of income, but they literally do cost more for the poor than for others.

The BOP refers to the four-billion-plus people living on less than US$1,500 per year[23], with more than half of them being women[24]. We have illustrated this in the 'Pyramid' below (see Figure 3).

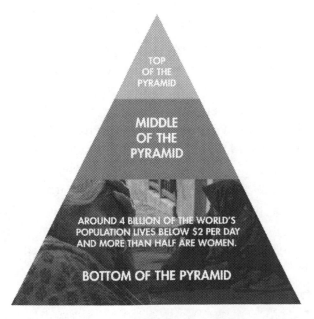

TOP
OF THE
PYRAMID

MIDDLE
OF THE
PYRAMID

AROUND 4 BILLION OF THE WORLD'S
POPULATION LIVES BELOW $2 PER DAY
AND MORE THAN HALF ARE WOMEN.

BOTTOM OF THE PYRAMID

Figure 3

3

The BOP Penalty manifests itself in several ways:

There is an objective increase in the price of goods and services, because it is more expensive to transport them there. For example, a sack of cement costs US$6 on Indonesia's richest and most populated island, Java. In its poorest region, Papua, the same sack of cement can cost more than a staggering US$150.[25] This deprives Papua of the economic opportunities that the people on Java have. But this is not a deliberate plot. Papua's remote location makes it expensive for goods to be transported there. And because the people are too poor to buy much, there are no economies of scale. Also, there are hardly any factories in Papua producing large quantities of items to sell to the rest of the world, so the ships sending goods to Papua have to return empty, with the shipping company charging double to cover the empty return trip. As a result, people are discouraged from sending goods to Papua, and when goods are scarce, sellers end up charging more for them—even way above the extra shipping costs that they incur. It is a vicious cycle.

Mainstream options are not available to very poor people, so they have to use less conventional, and more expensive, options. Take electricity, for example. It extends a family's productive day beyond nightfall, enabling children to study for longer periods of time and parents to do extra work, like weaving, to earn more money. However, very poor communities are much less likely to have access to a national power grid. Even in cities, self-built homes or slums are not connected to the electricity grid. Remote rural areas are even less likely to be connected. So the communities with the least money end up spending five times more for energy than richer people who can afford to pay the local energy company regularly for their connection to the grid. The people who can least afford it will have to use diesel fuel or kerosene just to power generators, or light lamps and stoves, while paying more for it, given the cost to get it to them. Those with more money make smaller and regular payments and receive clean electricity straight to their homes: powering refrigerators, televisions, computers, printers, internet connections—things that help them remain more educated, better-fed and better-informed than the very poorest. Ironically, the poor are paying more for fuel and kerosene's 'dirty' energy, which is ruinous to health and leads to even greater costs.

People with money are given better resources to optimally manage their finances. Many privileges are given to people with even a modest amount of money. They are able to put their money in a bank, acquire insurance, receive a credit card and obtain a loan or mortgage. In short, they have a range of options to avail of when money is tight. They can pay for something big in instalments, or put their money in a savings account to keep themselves from the temptation to spend it, or pay upfront with a credit card and reimburse the charges when their salary comes in, or pay small monthly premiums to avoid forking out for a huge bill when they fall ill. As they have stable incomes, they can plan their lives better and have access to resources to manage their money more effectively.

What would do if you had nowhere to put your money and no access to emergency finances to smooth over the rough patches? Life is like that for the very poor. Until very recently, banks would not consider lending to the very poor as they earn either daily-rated wages, or as and when they get work. The banks do not consider it worthwhile to set up savings accounts for them because it would cost them more than the money to be made from their tiny deposits. The premiums for health insurance are out of the poor's league when they can barely spare money for preventive measures like chlorine for water purification, or mosquito nets to stave off malaria.

The poor have to rely on family, friends and moneylenders to manage their money. When they experience a family emergency, such as a death or serious illness, they are less likely to receive money from these friendly sources and so have to borrow from loan sharks. But the rate charged by loan sharks ranges from 40% to 200% per year[26]—far more than any standard bank or credit card. One striking example is a moneylender in Chennai who charges 4.69% interest per day, which could turn a US$5 loan into nearly US$100 million within a year. [27] It is a vicious cycle that keeps people in crippling poverty.

Savings cooperatives (where available) are far better as they do not charge any interest; it is simply a matter of everyone putting in a small amount and the total sum being disbursed to one person at a time, in turns.

There is also a mental manifestation of the BOP Penalty—the poor accept it as their lot, so they tend not to plan, or make investments for the future.

While we feel sad for people who live in very poor communities and wish life could be better for them, they view their circumstances as plain and simple reality, which in itself keeps them locked in this cycle of poverty.

"I grew up watching British news programmes feature elderly African women carrying big bundles of wood on their heads to convey the tragic poverty of a continent that should be helped and pitied. But when I went to Nigeria, I found that to these women, it was just normal. These women would not be dreaming to have a cart or someone to carry it for them, or not cook with wood at all—as these options would seem like a ridiculous extravagance. Just as I would consider it a ridiculous extravagance if someone had suggested having a live-in maid so I wouldn't have to clean my flat, or hiring a personal shopper as I don't like buying clothes. I'm not rich enough to do that. To those women in Nigeria, the idea that their lives could be so different that they wouldn't need to carry wood on their heads was just as absurd. In Nigeria, I realised that however poor you are, your life is your life and you just get on with it." – Lizzy Hawkins

Meanwhile, people tend to hold poor people to far higher standards than they themselves would adhere to. While slurping on a pricey disposable cup of coffee, they might say that poor people should not spend scarce pennies on sugary tea or cigarettes as the money could go towards extra products to sell in their small shops, or towards their children's school fees. They prejudge that the poor are poor because they are lazy or do not know how to use their money wisely.

But that attitude is premised on poor people believing that they will have a bit of money to save the following week, and the week after that, until they accumulate the requisite sum. But in their experience, they will not amass that money; something will happen to derail their life and plans. They might get sick and have no work for a few days. So there is no point saving because they would never reach a point where those savings would amount to anything, or so they believe.

We all do this.

We are very bad at making sacrifices in the present for some future benefit—particularly if we do not really believe that the benefit will occur. Why is it so hard to stick to diets, sacrificing tasty food in the present, for the future reward of a slimmer figure (which will never be slim enough) or to exercise, sacrificing comfort and entertainment now, for the future reward of better health (which we do not appreciate until we fall ill)?

So people who are very poor are even less likely to make long-term decisions because their lives can be so easily derailed by the smallest things. They earn money in a way that is extremely vulnerable to shocks. They may run tiny businesses in poor communities, so they make hardly any money. They could be day labourers and cannot rely on getting work every day. They might work on farms, which are susceptible to drought, disease and price fluctuations. So they make decisions based on worst-case scenarios and assume that any massive change to their lives will take too long, too much effort and probably not succeed anyway.

Finally, life is more costly for the poorest people in the world because they have to make a lot more decisions with a lot less access to information for the right choices. So they have to pay the cost of bad judgements—or procrastinating and not acting in time—far more than people who have those decisions made for them. Abhijit Banerjee and Esther Duflo explain the additional burden of decision-making borne by the very poor in their excellent book about poverty, *Poor Economics.* This book, which synthesises decades of scientific studies among the world's poorest, is well worth reading.

> *First, the poor often lack critical pieces of information and believe things that are not true. They are unsure about the benefits of immunising children; they think there is little value in what is learned in the first few years of education; they don't know how much fertiliser they need to use; they don't know which is the easiest way to get infected with HIV; they don't know what their politicians do when in office. When their firmly held beliefs turn out to be incorrect, they end up making the wrong decision, sometimes with drastic consequences...*
>
> *Second, the poor bear responsibility for too many aspects of their lives. The richer you are, the more the 'right' decisions are made for you. The poor have no piped water, and therefore, do not benefit from the chlorine that city government puts into the*

water supply. If they want clean drinking water, they have to purify it themselves. They cannot afford ready-made breakfast cereals and therefore have to make sure that they and their children get enough nutrients. They have no automatic way to save, such as a retirement plan or a contribution to Social Security, so they have to find a way to make sure that they save. These decisions are difficult for everyone because they require some thinking now or some other small cost today, and the benefits are usually reaped in the distant future. As such, procrastination very easily gets in the way. For the poor, this is compounded by the fact that their lives are already much more demanding than ours. Many of them run small businesses in highly competitive industries; most of the rest work as casual laborers and need to constantly worry about where their next job will come from.

– Abhijit Banerjee and Esther Duflo in
'Poor Economics', pp.268-269[28]

"It makes me angry to see people being exploited or pushed into a corner through no fault of their own. We need people to champion their cause. I feel so passionately about this because I have been blessed with many benefactors. I stand on the shoulders of these giants. I have to pass it on because these opportunities are a responsibility; that's my simple philosophy." – Audrey Tan

"One remarkable section of Professor Muhammad Yunus' book, 'Creating a World Without Poverty', describes a world where poverty only exists in museums. 'Once poverty is gone, we'll need to build museums to display its horrors to future generations. They'll wonder why poverty continued so long in human society—how a few people could live in luxury while billions dwelt in misery, deprivation and despair.' I could not imagine my children and grandchildren looking me in the eye and asking me how I could have tolerated seeing people live in those circumstances and if I did something to end poverty. There are days when I wonder how different my life would have been if my parents had not immigrated to Singapore. This book really caused me to jump up and ask myself what I could do to help end poverty." – Laina Raveendran Greene

We have a choice here. As a world, we can choose to accept poverty as a fact of life, or we can believe that poverty can be eliminated.

Make no mistake, it matters whether we believe this or not. If we believe that we can end poverty, we will make different decisions. We will commit more wholeheartedly to a world where we care more about the social and environmental impact of our actions. We will be braver when arguing with cynics who think that we are fools and that the only thing that matters is the financial bottom line. Belief is a choice. It takes more courage to believe in a world that can be better, because then we have to act like the world is better. And if more and more of us act like the world is better, then it will be. It is up to us.

We can end poverty. The evidence exists and you can use it to confront the people who say it is not possible. Ever since 189 countries joined together in 2000 to commit to the United Nations Millennium Development Goals, they have made astonishing progress. Extreme poverty rates have been more than halved since 1990. The proportion of undernourished people in the developing regions of the world has fallen by almost half. The primary school enrolment rate in developing regions has reached 91 percent, and many more girls are now in school compared to 15 years ago. The under-five mortality rate has declined by more than half, and maternal mortality is down 45 percent worldwide. The proportion of people who lack access to improved sources of water has been halved.[29]

This proves that we can do it. Mankind created poverty and mankind can, and must, end it. The new UN Sustainable Development Goals (SDGs) are more ambitious than before and Goal Number One is to end poverty. This time, 196 countries signed up to the UN SDGs.[30] And as more people around the world become richer, more people are mobilising their money to achieve those goals, from Jet Li, to Bill Gates, Warren Buffet, JK Rowling, and many more.

Poverty is a multi-pronged problem. Those of us who are in a position to help have a choice: we can either accept that these problems are too entrenched, too big for us to shift, and so we turn away; or we can acknowledge that poverty is man-made and so we can end it for good.

It is very easy to turn away and pretend you are not affected by poverty. We can continue with our lives and tell ourselves that our monthly charitable donations are enough and there is nothing more we can do.

But you know that is wrong. That is why you are reading this book. You are searching for a way to change lives for the better. You want to use your privileges and resources to help.

You have to act.

What We Have Learnt

- Poverty is about having no good options. It means hunger, lack of education, poor health and shorter life expectancy.
- Life is more expensive for the very poor. This is manifested in a phenomenon known as the Bottom of the Pyramid Penalty (BOP Penalty). The BOP sees the very poor paying more for the same goods than others, and making decisions with less access to information for the right choices.
- While global poverty might seem like a huge problem, small acts can cause ripple effects for huge impact. Humility is important to help us understand the reality of the problems so we can find the best solutions.
- We can end poverty if we commit to eradicating it. Nations have made good progress in addressing the UN Millennium Development Goals and there is potential to achieve more impact through the newer UN Sustainable Development Goals (SDGs).

CHAPTER 2

THE ANATOMY OF POVERTY

"Overcoming poverty is not a task of charity, it is an act of justice. Like slavery and apartheid, poverty is not natural. It is man-made and it can be overcome and eradicated by the actions of human beings... Sometimes it falls on a generation to be great. YOU can be that great generation. Let your greatness blossom."
– Nelson Mandela[31]

Everyone has something that ignites their passion and you may be thinking that poverty is not your issue. It could be women's rights, education, the destruction of the rainforest, or access to water. You may be worried about things closer to home and looking for solutions to those problems—crime, disease, or job losses.

Most of these issues are linked to poverty. We are passionate about eradicating poverty because it exacerbates most of the other issues you may be more passionate about. Poverty is linked to crime, to deforestation, to people becoming refugees, to corruption, to slow economic growth, and even to the spread of disease. Poverty affects us all and is bad for everyone.

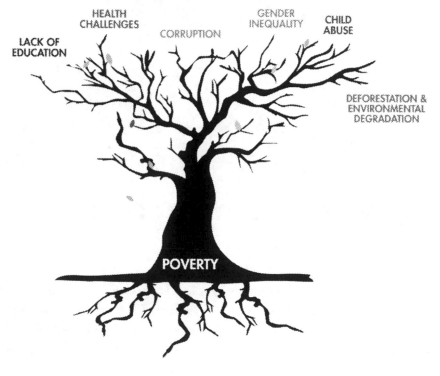

POVERTY ROOT CAUSE OF SOCIETY ILLS

Figure 4

Deforestation and Poverty

Every year, 13 million hectares of forest are destroyed.[32] That is almost the size of Bangladesh.[33] Every year!

Since 1990, an area of forest the size of South Africa has been lost.[34] The loss of our forests is accelerating climate change and extinguishing whole species of plants and animals from the planet.[35]

Poverty is largely to be blamed for these and many other issues. Around half of all timber which is taken from forests illegally, is taken for fuel—to boil water, heat homes and cook food.[36] A further unknown amount is lost because small farmers burn the forest to grow crops. For example, in Indonesia, small-scale farmers burn rainforests to plant palm oil, which they sell to large palm oil producers.[37] The best-known victims of this deforestation are orangutans—beautiful, human-like forest-dwellers.

But animals are not the only victims. The impoverished suffer because of this destruction too. 1.6 billion people around the world rely on forests for food, water, shelter, medicine and clothing.[38] But without better options, people in poverty will continue to contribute to deforestation. This is the irony of poverty.

Corruption and Poverty

Corruption is a disease, which makes everything worse. It makes infrastructure collapse because bad companies pay bribes to win projects, or inferior products are used so someone can skim off the remaining cash. It makes public services worse when public servants learn that they can earn money by doing their jobs poorly, and then putting a hand out under the table to do it well. It makes governments ineffective when politicians can be bribed not to do what is best for their country.

Study after study has shown a strong link between poverty and corruption. Corruption hits the poor disproportionately hard. It makes them even poorer, because the bribes are a much bigger proportion of their income than for richer people. And they do have to pay, because otherwise, they will not receive vital goods and services. They have to bribe their way past the roadblock to reach the market and sell their goods. They have to pay a bribe for the medicines they need. They have to pay bribe after bribe to be educated. And they have to pay bribe after bribe after bribe to even get a job, let alone get 'justice'—which is no justice at all because the person who pays the most wins.

Poverty robs the poor of their voice in a corrupt system. And it compels people to participate in the very system of corruption that robs them.

Poverty and children's rights

A UNICEF report in 2004 titled *The State of the World's Children*[39] stated that:

- Over 90 million children are severely malnourished.
- 400 million children do not have access to safe drinking water.
- 500 million children do not have access to a toilet.
- 270 million children do not have access to health services, including basic treatment for diarrhoea and vaccinations for the most common diseases.
- 640 million children do not have access to proper shelter.
- 140 million children have never been to school.
- 448 million are deprived of information about the outside world, whether through TV, radio or newspapers.

These deprived children are products of poverty. No parent wants their child to be hungry, sick, and cold; just as your parents did not want it for you, and you do not want it for your children.

It is no different for people in poverty. The difference is that they have no choice. No parent wants to send their child to beg in the streets. No parent wants to send their child to work in a factory. But poverty compels them to, because they have no better options.

Poverty and women's rights

The impact of poverty is much greater on women than men (the feminisation of poverty)

Women suffer more, partly because of their bodies—women can get pregnant, making them far more vulnerable to sickness and death. Pregnancy and childbirth are cataclysmic physical events that put women's bodies at great risk. It is easy to forget that in places where women are able to afford hygienic healthcare. Medical complications from pregnancy and childbirth are the leading cause of death among adolescent girls in developing countries. Women living in sub-Saharan Africa have a 1-in-36 risk of dying in pregnancy or childbirth in their lifetime. The odds are merely 1-in-4,900 in a developed country.[40]

Poverty does not just mean that women are more likely to die earlier or be more ill. A family in poverty is less able to afford schooling for their children, and when faced with the hard decision of whom to educate, they would pick the boys. So ultimately, women are less likely to receive secondary school education than men anywhere in the world. 62 million girls miss out on school and women make up two-thirds of the world's illiterate population.[41] When women do not attend secondary school, they will likely marry early, become pregnant earlier and face the terrible health risks of pregnancy and even die earlier. That is an appalling waste of human resources and talent!

On top of being deprived of a decent education and being more vulnerable to sickness and death, women are far less likely to be paid for their work. Women and girls can spend up to five hours a day collecting fuel and up to four hours a day cooking. In some low-income countries, women and girls spend 40 billion hours a year collecting water—the equivalent of one year's labour by France's entire workforce.[42]

This is caused by not just poverty but also centuries of social attitudes that devalue women. There is no rational, objective reason for not educating women or not paying them for work. But, as we have said earlier, poverty is about having no good choices. If you cannot afford to send all your children to school, and you know that employers do not like to employ women as much as men, then you will not waste money educating a girl over a boy.

The feminisation of poverty also leads to very specific abuse of women's rights. Every year, 15 million girls are married before the age of 18. That is 28 every minute.[43] When a girl marries young, she sets back her whole country's development. She is more likely to be taken out of school, become pregnant too young and suffer from complications; childbirth is one of the leading causes of death for girls aged 15-19 in low and middle-income countries.[44] She is less likely to have any decision-making power because she has had no choice in whom she marries. She is more likely to suffer violence and describe her first sexual experience as 'forced'.

Poverty is not the only reason that child marriage happens, but it is a powerful driver. Girls from poor families are twice more likely to be married before the age of 18 than girls from richer families.[45] Since women are less likely to earn money, more likely to have health problems and traditionally believed to be less valuable than men, poor families may choose to marry them off young because they cannot afford to raise them. Some are even forced to sell them to the highest bidder even when they know this could mean modern day slavery, or worse, for their child. They want to believe that marriage gives them better prospects than remaining at home, or they just need the money to help the other children they have. Again, these are the awful choices faced by people in poverty. 'Marry her off, and your daughter might live a better life than the one you could offer'. But that is unlikely. Girls from poor families who marry young stay poor, whereas for every year a girl stays in secondary school, she will eventually earn 15-25% more than if she had left earlier.[46] Marrying young will leave her poorer, less educated, and she will have no voice to protest when it is her daughter's turn.

As a result, we have lost the potential for an estimated 865 million women worldwide to contribute more fully in the labour force. 865 million is more than double the United States' population. 812 million of those women live in emerging and developing nations that need all the economic power they can build up.[47] That is part of the reason that we need to focus on women if we want to effectively eradicate poverty.

So for Angels of Impact, if we want to focus on eradication of poverty, it makes sense that we focus on women. The other reason for focussing on women is far more positive; women are great investments and can make greater impact on poverty than men.

Invest in Women to end poverty effectively!

If you are a man reading this book, please do not feel affronted that we are focussing on women. We are thrilled to have you read this book and want you to be part of this mission just as much as women. We welcome anyone who is committed to our mission.

Men should not feel marginalised, as that does not help us create an inclusive and prosperous world. If we want to end poverty we must focus on the majority of the poor, who are women.

Women have a greater role in reducing poverty than men. When women have access to money, they are much more likely to channel it to their families' health and wellbeing—creating a virtuous cycle that multiplies through generations. These are not mere sexist claims; we have included an extensive list of sources on this in our 'Further Reading' section at the end of this book. So do not just take it from us; discover the evidence for yourself.

When women have control over household finances, they are likely to save more, their children are likely to be better nourished and they are more inclined to invest in their children's education.[48] The United Nations Development Programme found that when women control household income, the impact on their children's health is twenty times greater than when a man controls that income.[49] Why is this an incredible statistic? Well, it is rare to find a situation in which all experts come to a consensus, so to have them all agree that something accounted for 50% of change is a massive statement.

Different studies have found that women with more control over resources is linked to the following: improved health in pre-school children (Bangladesh); use of mosquito nets in malarial areas (Benin); better child nutrition (Brazil); and, higher likelihood of children being vaccinated (India), among others.[50]

There was a rather heart-breaking study in Bangladesh[51] that examined whether hailing from larger families affected children's health. It found that the children's health was unaffected, but the mothers were shorter and weighed less than women with fewer children. They had gone without food so that their children could eat. That is the extent to which women will sacrifice themselves for their families.

Investing in women has huge economic impact. Consider this; in the developing world, 16% less women than men use the Internet. If an additional 600 million women and girls gained access to the Internet in the next three years, GDP across 144 developing countries could be boosted by up to US$13-18 billion.[52]

If that is too abstract a number, let us break it down: that is an average of US$90-$125 million per country—simply by giving women access to the Internet. Think of the college education, healthcare and electricity you can buy with that much money! So if we can help 865 million women[53] to participate more fully in the workforce and fulfil their potential, we will have a far better world.

And there is more!

Women are not just a 'pity' investment. Women are often *better* investments than men. Grameen Bank, the world's best-known microfinance bank, lends exclusively to women. Its loan repayment rate is an enviable 98%.[54] Grameen pioneered the microfinance model in Bangladesh and found, through decades of trial and error, that women invested their loans in their families' upliftment, while men generally spent the money on themselves. On the other side of the world, women-led private technology companies in Silicon Valley achieved a 35% higher return on investment, and, when venture-backed, brought in 12% higher revenue than male-owned tech companies.[55]

More broadly, venture capital firms investing in women-led businesses secured better returns than the firms that only invested in men.[56] And companies run by women—especially small and medium-sized companies (SMEs)—are just as good at repaying loans as companies run by men.[57]

Added to that, women entrepreneurs have their own virtuous circles. Women who run businesses are more likely to employ other women—about 85% of women-owned SMEs have women in senior management compared to approximately 10% of SMEs owned by men.[58] Bill Gates said when he placed women and girls at the heart of the Bill and Melinda Gates Foundation's work, "Empowering women and girls to transform their lives is one of the smartest investments we can make".[59]

Sorry gents, but the facts speak for themselves. It may just be the fault of the system that women suffer the most, yet women are indeed better investments so they can be more effective tools to overcome poverty. It only makes sense to invest where one gets more return on nvestment (ROI).

What We Have Learnt

- Global poverty is an entrenched and multi-pronged problem. The world's poorest pay more than they should for basic products and services that richer people take for granted.
- The very poor bear a greater burden of responsibility for their lives, without having the tools to make good decisions.
- Women are poverty's greatest victims through a phenomenon known as the feminisation of poverty. Women receive less education, are less likely to be paid for their work, more likely to be ill, and more likely to die earlier.
- Women are great investments. When women have access to money, they are much more likely to channel it to their families' health and wellbeing—creating a virtuous cycle that multiplies through generations.

CHAPTER 3

SERVE, NOT SAVE, THE POOR

"It's very vulgar to think of the poor as a market. Even to think of the poor only as beneficiaries, or the poor as consumers. We don't look at the poor as partners, we don't look at the poor as employers, we don't look at the poor as asset creators, and we don't look at the poor as solution providers. And that is part of the problem of why we can't end poverty." – Harish Hande, Founder of SELCO [60]

We know that we can end poverty, but how do we begin?

It is important not to want to *save* the poor, but rather to *serve* them. We need to be humble, listen to, respect and embrace the solutions offered by the very people who are most affected by poverty. The poor deserve the right to be treated with dignity, and credited with having innovative solutions to their own problems.

Poor people have good reasons for their decisions. To really change their lives, we need to understand and respect their decisions and their reasons.

If you have never experienced poverty, it is easy to see the poor as helpless victims or as people not working hard enough. As we said before, people living in poverty are dealing with no access to clean water, or clean and cheap electricity, or education; they live in poor health and the constant stress of juggling an arsenal of challenges, in the absence of good role models. One could simply look at those challenges and think, "Surely, if they could help themselves, they would have escaped such a relentlessly painful existence?"

But that line of thinking not only underestimates the complexity of their challenges, it undermines the poor themselves. Despite these huge challenges, people who are poor come up with ways to survive— their methods may not be good for their health, may be frowned upon or even illegal—but they will do what they need to do. For example, women, men and children scavenge waste in several countries: from the elderly, homeless man rummaging for discarded food in the bins on a British high street, to an Indonesian woman fishing out plastic bottles from a rubbish-choked river to sell for a handful of rupiahs. It is dirty and dangerous, and no poverty alleviation programme would ever recommend it. The fact that it still happens shows that people who are poor have to find their own ways to survive—ways that people who are not impoverished would never consider.

"When I visited Jakarta, I asked why there were so many dumpsters and slum-dwellers. The answer is complex, but one element is caused by poor returns from agriculture or climate change, which pushes people to move into cities and end up in slums. Ironically, surfing dumpsters for things to sell gives them a better income than farming. The dumpsters can yield so much because there's all this waste in city centres from people who have things in abundance. It's a warped cycle; increasing consumption creates all these side effects."– Audrey Tan

"A two-week visit to Nigeria in 2009 shifted my perspective on poverty. Nigeria's capital, Abuja, contained wealthy enclaves populated by aid workers, diplomats, and oil workers. But elsewhere, the country was built on the assumption that nobody had very much. My friend had picked me up from the airport and I looked out of the windows at the muddy, single-storey one-room buildings with corrugated iron roofs or reclaimed wood and thought, 'Ah, these must be the slums. I wonder when we'll get into the

main city.' After half an hour, I realised that these 'slums' were the city. Once I'd grasped that what ordinary Nigerians had was less than even the poor's lot in the UK, everything made more sense. You drank a (warm) bottle of Coke next to the vendor because they wanted their bottle back to earn a few cents from returning it. When you took a bus, you waited hours until it was full— there were no specific departure times because no one could afford empty seats. When your bus (or, in this case, estate car with an extra row of seats crammed in) broke down on the road, you had to hope your driver was a good mechanic because, otherwise, the twelve of you would have to rely on getting lifts from passing vehicles—most of which would be as full as yours had been. Meals consisted mainly of rice or maize and people rarely had meat, as it was expensive and seen as a luxury. The national power company, NEPA, was cheerfully nicknamed 'Never Expect Power Always'. You went to bed when it got dark or you wasted expensive batteries. When the water ran, everyone dragged huge tubs of water to the tap, and clay water filters were ubiquitous.

"Yet life went on. I remember the reaction of a group of men when I told them that people in Europe pay hundreds of dollars to travel to places where they could just lie in the sun. 'What? That sun up there?' one man asked, pointing out of the window. Then they burst into uncontrollable laughter. In Nigeria, far more than in the homeless shelters in London, I learnt that people who live in poverty don't consider themselves poor and they don't gratefully submit to the ministrations of some benevolent power. They look at what they have and use it as best they can. Just like everyone else." – Lizzy Hawkins

If you do not understand or empathise with why poor people do what they do, you cannot serve them.

Too many organisations—from multi-national NGOs to well-meaning charities—approach problems through their own lenses and come with pre-existing solutions, which often do not fit the reality of a local community. For example, people love donating to organisations that provide clean water in the developing world. In theory, this is an obvious way to improve the lives of the poor as it reduces water-borne diseases and frees up time for work or education instead of spending it on fetching water from far away. But sadly, new technology is often brought into communities without explaining how it works, or how to fix it, or the technology uses parts that are not available in the area for replacements when they break down. For a while, pumps powered by children playing on them were hugely popular. Yet often, children do not have time to play as they are busy working in the fields or people are too malnourished to have the energy to use them. Instead, local solutions are abundant and bringing in donated equipment from outside kills local innovation since it is hard to compete with free.

There have also been cases where wells were built without teaching the community about bacteria, disease and the importance of clean water—things that even the most scientifically advanced countries only discovered relatively recently after centuries of scientific research and millions of deaths! Without understanding hygiene, without functioning latrines, without knowing about the importance of washing hands, the wells quickly became contaminated or ruined through lack of maintenance.

People who are poor are innovative and make smart choices to stay alive. Often, their perspective of the world is very different from those trying to help them. The history of poverty alleviation is littered with examples of solutions that have been provided without fully understanding why the people being helped act the way they do.

International Development Enterprises Ltd.'s (ide) CEO, Paul Polka, gives an excellent example of why it is important to understand how the people they are trying to help actually think:

In the 1990s, agriculture experts in Bangladesh were dismayed that small-acreage farmers were applying only a tiny fraction of the fertiliser that their monsoon-season rice crops needed, whereas using the recommended amount would increase their rice yields, thus, tripling their investment in the fertiliser. The experts complained about the irrational and superstitious behaviour of small-acreage farmers, and set up extension programmes and farmer-training programmes, but nothing worked. The farmers continued to apply a tiny fraction of the fertiliser that their rice needed to thrive. Finally, somebody asked some farmers why they were doing that.

"Oh, that's easy," they said. "Every ten years or so around here, there is a major flood during the monsoon season that carries away all the fertiliser we apply. So we only apply the amount of fertiliser we can afford to lose in a tenth-year flood."

Here is another example of how solutions can have unintended consequences, and how these unintended consequences better reflect the priorities, as opposed to the needs, of a community. This is a great example of how local experts may actually know more or have very rational reasons for what they do.

Mosquito nets are distributed across Africa to help prevent malaria. But communities living by the sea, lakes and rivers use them as fishing nets. If you think, "That's terrible! Those nets are meant to help prevent a potentially fatal illness!" think again. Those families have to choose between the risk of a disease in the future, which could be treated and cured, and the immediate reality of watching their children and family go hungry, suffer from stunted growth or malnourishment.

People who are poor—like people everywhere—will use whatever resources they can get their hands on. The Musana Community Development Organisation in Uganda was co-founded as a home for 80 orphans. Co-founder Leah Pauline reported, "Soon after creating the home, we discovered that our 'orphans' had parents and relatives who loved them. These parents were willing to leave their children at our door in the belief that outside help would give their children the chance at a better life".[61] With this realisation and understanding, Musana started partnering and collaborating with local Iganga community members to create businesses that can generate income to fund other outreach projects, so that the children can remain with their own families.

"I had visited the MS Swaminathan Research Foundation's Knowledge Centres set up in Indian temples and rural areas for people to access the Internet. Interestingly, these centres were run by local women, with not a lot of education—maybe basic primary school education at most. I was amazed, because the women maintained the computers and the solar panels that powered the centres. Why did they want to run the Knowledge Centre? 'For our children,' they said. They were willing to learn, for their children and ran classes on how to use the computers for the children after

school. The best part was that they even created applications using Excel spreadsheets for the local dairywomen to manage their accounts. These innovations came from the women. I visited them over time to ask how they were doing, and they would say, 'Well, my son is studying engineering, and my daughter is doing such-and-such'. How did they find out about these things? They'd say, 'Oh, I used the Internet and we found out about scholarships.' They just blew my mind. My interaction with those women really changed my mindset about how I perceived poverty and the poor.

"Later, when I visited Grameen Shakti in Bangladesh, I went to the most rural areas and saw women making mobile phone chargers; and soldering and making solar lamps by hand at home using kits. They were climbing onto roofs to fix solar panels and lighting up homes, still in their sarees. That's what transformed me. That's when I stopped thinking, 'Oh we've got to do something about poverty,' and instead thought, 'We've got to be partners with them.' They can do it, they just need access to the solar panels, or the funding, or maybe they're buying single pieces, which is expensive and actually need someone to bulk-buy for them. They're already doing it! All they need is for us to support what they're doing. My interactions with those women changed how I looked at the poor." – Laina Raveendran Greene

In the next section, we want to highlight to you incredible innovations from the world's poorest communities. We hope this will help you shift your perspective towards how you can serve the poor instead.

People's creativity and ingenuity may be harnessed with amazing results, regardless of how rich or poor they are. Here are some examples of spontaneous solutions that we find really inspiring.

MittiCool Fridge

Mansukhbhai Prajapati had lost almost all his stock of earthenware in the massive earthquake which had struck the Indian state of Gujarat in 2001. It was his second catastrophic loss; the first was the collapse of the Morbi dam in 1979, which killed 25,000 people and destroyed his family's possessions and forced them to move 30 kilometres away to rebuild their lives.[62] The only son of a clay craftsman,

Mansukhbhai had worked in a factory that made rooftop tiles. A few years later, he had become the owner of a factory making earthenware utensils. He helped in the relief effort following the 2001 Gujarat earthquake and donated whichever of his factory's products that were still intact. In the debris, he found a local newspaper that featured one of his clay pots lying broken, with the caption, "The broken fridge of the poor".[63] Inspiration struck. He knew that the pots were used to keep water cool—he had used them himself. He wondered if he could harness the cooling power of earthenware to create an affordable fridge for the poor without electricity.

After much trial and error, the MittiCool refrigerator was born. It looks like a modern fridge, but instead of electricity, it uses the cooling power of evaporation by slowly dripping water down the sides of the container. This cools the inside of the fridge, creating a safe and hygienic place to store food and water. The fridge retails at US$81[64] in a country where an electric fridge costs anything between US$300 and US$1,500[65]—not including the shattering, ongoing expense of electricity.

Figure 5. One of the models of the MittiCool refrigerator available for purchase on MittiCool's website. Source: MittiCool Refrigerator [Digital Image]. (2016). Reprinted with permission from: https://mitticool.com/product/mitticool-refrigerator/

William Kamkwamba

William Kamkwamba was a schoolboy in Malawi in 2001 when a famine arrived. "I was just a simple farmer in a country of poor farmers."[66] With the family barely surviving on three mouthfuls of nsima (maize meal) per day, they could no longer afford his school fees. Unable to attend classes, William started visiting the local library where he read books about science and physics, slowly learning English through the diagrams in the books. One day he found a book called 'Using Energy'.[67] It showed how to build a windmill to produce electricity, so his family would no longer need to pay for the expensive kerosene that lit their home, nor for pump water—the water his family's parched fields so desperately needed. So William built a windmill with materials he could find—blue gum trees, bicycle parts, and items collected from a local scrap yard. His first windmill powered four electric lights and two radios in his family's home. Since then, he has built a solar-powered water pump that supplied the first drinking water in his village and is building more windmills.

Figure 6. William Kamkwamba with a windmill he built. Source: William Kamkwamba [Digital Image]. (2013). Reprinted with permission from: http://www.williamkamkwamba.com/home.html

The Barefoot College

The Barefoot College in India gives village women the opportunity to become engineers. It takes in women from remote Indian villages and trains them in electronics and engineering, enabling them to install and maintain solar powered appliances, such as phone chargers, lights and stoves in their communities. Armed with training from the Barefoot College, the ladies were not content simply to reproduce what they had been taught. When they learned about the ills from cooking with smoky kerosene or wood in poorly ventilated houses, the Barefoot College graduates looked for a better solution. Using the principles they had learned, they designed a solar stove, which used reflective panels to create intense heat from the sun's rays. The stove is made from readily available materials. It is another example—like William Kwamkwamba— of what people can achieve when they have access to resources.

We need to stop thinking that people who are poor do not know what is best for them. If they appear to make bad decisions—marrying off their 13-year-old daughter or taking a loan at 1000% interest—it is not because they are too stupid to know better; it is because they have no better options. Anyone who wants to end poverty needs to treat the poor as partners, not passive victims. It is a case of a hand-up, not a hand-out.

The stories above are the direct result of the minds, hands and hard work of people who were poor and found ways to change their lives. But without money and education, it is always going to be more difficult to find the resources to transform their own lives. Education gives them a whole set of new tools to use, and money gives them time, the ability to buy equipment and hire people so that they can make big changes. Professor Muhammad Yunus refers to the poor as a 'bonsai tree' which comes from the same seed as a big tree but its growth is stunted by the small pot and resources with which it has to grow, rather than being from a bad seed.[68] Poor people are often the best innovators since 'necessity is the mother of invention', after all.

People who are close to, and understand, the issues of the poor in their communities can co-create solutions to make tremendous impact. The following examples show the incredible impact of technology when applied to solve real problems, with great context and understanding of the community the technology is intended for.

Raji Borthakur's TJay Smart Glove

If Tejas Borthakur's epilepsy had been diagnosed earlier, his development might not have been as badly affected. His mother, Raji, lived a comfortable life in Bangalore and was shocked that even with the medical care that she could afford, the doctors took so long to diagnose Tejas—or TJ, as he is usually known. So how much worse would it be for someone without the financial means?

Raji decided to act so that other mothers would not have to undergo what she did. She started researching epilepsy intensively, working out a way of improving diagnosis and detecting early warning signs of severe seizures like those that TJ had suffered. She learnt that the standard diagnostic test for epilepsy, the ECG, did not always work—it depended on patients exhibiting epileptic patterns during the scan, which did not often happen. So even families like hers, who could afford an ECG, might fail to get a diagnosis until significant damage had been done.

She created a lightweight glove that could help sufferers monitor their condition for an early diagnosis and early warning of severe seizures. She drew global attention upon reaching the final round of the 'Innovate for Digital India Challenge' and received support from Intel, to create her 'TJay Smart Glove'. The glove constantly monitors the wearer's electrical signals, and is considerably cheaper than a scan.[69] Raji is now developing her glove for commercial use. Ultimately, she wants to make sure that no child's brain is damaged due to his/her epileptic fits not being treated in time.

mPedigree

Bright Simons realised the power of activism while still in school. At his harsh Presbyterian boarding school, the older boys bullied the younger ones in the name of tradition. When he became Student Council President, Bright took a stand against the long-standing abuse. After winning a scholarship to study at Durham University, Bright decided to give up academic pursuits to seek a more practical path—determined to combine his technological knowledge with his activist roots to change the lives of Ghana's poor rural farmers.

He realised that by default, the farmers were using organic methods. But their products were not certified 'organic', and the farmers were therefore missing out on extra money. Bright developed a system that allowed buyers to trace the origin of their food via SMS within seconds and confirm if it was 'organic'. The technology was sound, but the business model faltered.

Then a whole new market opened up: pharmaceuticals. At least one in five packets of drugs sold in sub-Saharan Africa's pharmacies is fake. Hundreds of thousands of people die every year as a result. In 2013, 120,000 children died because of sub-standard malaria medication.[70] That is more than 300 every single day. Bright realised that his SMS authentication system could help shoppers check the authenticity of drugs. After successful pilots in Ghana and Nigeria, the big pharmaceutical companies approached Bright. mPedigree now works with giants like AstraZeneca and Sanofi in the pharma domain, as well as, regulatory organisations to add codes to drug packages.[71] The codes are scratched off and buyers text the code to confirm the drugs are genuine.

Since its founding in 2007, mPedigree codes are now found on more than a billion packets across industries and markets with a growth rate of 100 million packets per quarter (mPedigree, personal communication, April 27, 2017). The company has expanded to 12 countries across Africa and South Asia.[72] It has widened its reach beyond pharmaceuticals and is now authenticating products across a huge range of sectors, including automobile parts, agricultural seeds, fertilisers and cosmetics.

Figure 7. A customer using mPedigree's mobile app to text a code on a box of drugs to confirm if they are genuine. Source: mPedigree [Digital Image]. (n.d.). Reprinted Reprinted with permission from: http://mpedigree.net/

Alfredo Moser and the Liter of Light movement

This story demonstrates the synergies between an on-the-ground innovation in Brazil and people power in the Philippines.

The Philippines is susceptible to natural disasters. Like many Filipinos, Liter of Light founder, Illac Diaz, grew up helping out at relief centres after such disasters. After becoming an urban planner, he was frustrated that despite his skills, the only aid he could offer during disasters was to transport bags of food around. He searched for a better way to help.

He started by using his urban planning skills to make building materials from easily available objects; he found that plastic water bottles filled with mud and chicken feathers made good bricks. He worked with volunteers to build a school with those bricks. For windows, they filled the bottles with water instead of mud, to let light through.

Serendipitously, a volunteer mentioned that after one of Brazil's frequent power cuts, Brazilian mechanic, Alfredo Moser, had invented a light using discarded plastic bottles. He used a plastic bottle filled with water and bleach and fixed the bottles through the roof of his house with polyester resin. The light that entered the room was similar to that of a 40-60 watt electric bulb. Illac realised that this simple invention could bring light to people who lack electricity.

The Liter of Light movement was born. Originally starting with Alfredo Moser's light design, the movement taught communities how to make the simple lights. They lit up houses in the slums of Manila, which were so tightly packed that residents lived in perpetual darkness. Shortly afterwards, the Liter of Light team developed a simple solar-powered light using a copper board and five components which can be bought from any electrical goods store. Cooperatives of women now build the lights and sell them to the local communities for US$5 each.[73] This is far cheaper than the dangerous candles or kerosene they had been using previously.

Liter of Light grew an army of volunteers who would be ready to mass-create Liters of Light when the next disaster struck.

The acid test for their concept was 2013's Typhoon Haiyan. Within days, 5,000 Liter of Light volunteers had made millions of solar lights for the communities who had lost everything in the disaster[74]—a task that would have taken months using relief agencies' traditional supply networks. The Liter of Light movement now has chapters across the world and has installed more than 350,000 bottle lights in over 15 countries— including some UN refugee camps.[75]

Illac Diaz is passionate about ground-up solutions. A huge part of Liter of Light's success, he says, comes from "the untapped people"— the "genius of the poor". In a 2015 interview, he said, "One of the greatest surprises is that when we taught them how to make solar lights, we learnt [from them] how to make street lights and fishing lights."[76]

Figure 8. A shopkeeper in her shop powered by a Liter of Light bottle light. Source: Liter of Light [Digital Image]. (2015).Reprinted with permission from: http://literoflight.org/index.php

Winsenga

Ugandans Joshua Okello, Aaron Tushabe and Josiah Kuvuma were college students conceiving a project for the 'Windows Imagine Cup', Microsoft's international student technology competition. They thought about life in Uganda and the difference in medical care between its city hospitals and remote villages. Every *minute, a woman dies from pregnancy and childbirth-related complications. 99% of those deaths happen in Sub-Saharan Africa[77], the region in which Joshua, Aaron and Josiah grew up. In the villages and towns of Uganda, pregnant women rely on 'sengas', local midwives, throughout their pregnancy. Without access to medical technology like ultrasound machines, the midwives relied on monitoring birth with a pinard horn, a conical device to listen to sounds in the womb. Skilled midwives could interpret the sounds, but such skills took years to learn and while sengas learned their craft, women were dying. The boys worked out that a mobile app coupled with the pinard horn would enable even less experienced midwives to give quality antenatal care.*

The boys worked with hospitals, midwives and medical experts to develop a mobile foetal heart rate monitor; a souped-up pinard horn with a sensitive microphone in it, plugged to a mobile phone. Called Winsenga, the app picks up the baby's heartbeat, diagnoses its health and gives the mother and midwives suggestions on how to treat any problems. The device enables sengas to visit mothers in their homes, rather than having mothers make the time-consuming, tiring journey into town.

Grameen Danone

Grameen Danone is a social business—a very specific type of social enterprise— that aims to improve the nutrition of children in Bangladesh by selling fortified yoghurt to the poor. The interesting element here is that despite diligent research, things started to go wrong for them. However, they found a way to turn this around.

Grameen Danone is a partnership between Grameen, which runs several social businesses in Bangladesh, and the global food giant, Danone. When it was set up, the Grameen Danone team conducted extensive research to develop the business model. The yoghurt was well received after its launch, but sales were flat.[78] It took months for the company to understand why.

It turned out that Grameen Danone had made some inaccurate assumptions. They had expected to sell plenty of yoghurt through their existing network of 'Grameen Ladies', women who were part of Grameen Bank's microfinance borrowers. These women had borrowed small amounts to set up small enterprises—basket weaving, cultivating vegetable plots, raising poultry, making dresses etc. Grameen Danone had taught them about the benefits of their yoghurt, given them insulated bags to carry the yoghurt in, explained how much commission they would earn, and waited for the sales to roll in.

They did not. At best, only 30 ladies were selling the yoghurt.[79] Many would sign up for a few days and then quit. Grameen Danone's response saved the day. They spoke to people on the ground and asked, "What have we done wrong?" The people on the ground gave them the answer. Grameen Danone had ignored a crucial cultural barrier. In rural Bangladesh, women stay close to home. While it is fine to be a Grameen Lady establishing a business out of your own home, door-to-door sales is completely different. It is unconventional and invites disapproval from the wider village—and in many cases, the women's husbands as well. It did not matter that she would be bringing in extra money. The social pressures were too strong.

Someone who supports gender equality and believes that people should not be treated differently simply because they were born female might argue that the husbands should tolerate the door-to-door sales and ignore the disapproval. But that attitude dismisses the priorities of the people you are trying to serve. Real impact comes from understanding what is important to them and designing a solution that will address that. Grameen Danone did that. Armed with this new understanding, they redesigned their recruitment process. They involved the women's families, made sure that husbands understood the benefits of their wives working and supported them doing it. In six months, the number of yoghurt sales ladies jumped from 27 to 270.[80] The impact on the women's lives was far greater because Grameen Danone had taken the effort to make their solution work on the ground.

Humility—understanding what is important to people, and respecting the decisions they make—can be a really difficult thing to practise. We often think that we have answers to people's problems. Then when they tell us the issue that is most important to them, it is so tempting to say, "But why are you worrying about this when it's so obvious that this other thing is causing you far bigger difficulties?" It can even be painful to watch. When you start working with people who are very poor, you will see that they face such a multitude of issues that it is very difficult to know where to start. That is why humility will be your strongest asset; by listening and understanding people's real needs, we can get a better idea of where we need to start, even if it is not the starting point we would have chosen.

The three of us have each learnt the need to put our own assumptions aside when trying to serve people living in poverty.

"A homeless shelter I worked in held classes for the guests. I was scornful of the list, 'Hat-making? Puppetry? Singing? What use is that? We should be teaching the guests practical skills, not fluff!' I remained sceptical until I heard one of the shelter's choirs sing in a concert. I still get tears in my eyes at the memory. People whom I knew as erratic, aggressive, or silent, were smiling broadly as they sang on stage. Their faces filled with pride and joy as they stood through a standing ovation. I had thought that they needed practical skills (and I still think I was right). But I hadn't realised how important it was for them to do something that they loved, something they could be proud of, which gave them stability and routine where they had none. To receive a standing ovation for their own work and effort, when they were used to being dismissed as despicable, scrounging burdens, did far more for their self-respect and determination than any number of classes in bike repair or plumbing." – Lizzy Hawkins

Laina had her own epiphany about implementing solutions for poverty alleviation.

"After having lived in Switzerland and the US, I became very technology-driven. I was working in INTELSAT, so I thought, 'Introduce satellite bandwidth and it'll solve all their problems!' Or, 'If only they had knowledge centres, they would have better access to e-learning. If only they had the Internet, their lives would be transformed by access to information!'

"Then you begin to realise that people don't even have electricity, so how can they use the Internet or their cell phones? They have to walk one hour to the nearest market to charge their phone, and that's one hour away from feeding their family or productive life.

"I learnt that technology for good has to be in partnership with the community. Introducing the Internet could mean new problems such as wasting time on pornography or other useless endeavours. Involving the women in the community in access provision, meant the women became the censors. Women also helped lower the cost of bringing technology to the villages. Women working with Grameen Shakti are climbing up homes and installing solar panels in remote Bangladeshi villages. Some people might say that their installation isn't very good, but they are right there in the community. You may have a very skilled solar engineer, but if there's no road, then he can't get there, or if it will cost too much, then he's of no use.

"I saw communities bring their own Internet to their villages and innovative technologies such as using open-mesh Wifi. I'd wondered at first, 'With all the state-of-the art Wifi systems, why not use them instead?' I learnt that the villagers' solutions were cheaper and better at making the most of lesser resources. Even when people in developed countries had Wifi issues, they began to use mesh Wifi too. I learnt that the missing solution wasn't only technology; it was the innovative business models, financing models, and basically community ownership to keep technology working. Having community ownership and involvement meant better and more sustainable solutions. In some places where solar panels were donated, the panels become coffee tables, because there was no ownership or understanding of their value or they were sold to help feed the family. With SELCO, they have to pay for them—paying what they would otherwise have forked out for kerosene—so there's ownership and they clean the panels, look after them and even know how to maintain them. They saw the value of how the solar panels helped increase their own value. That the power of community involvement in offering new products and services, no matter how small, could make a huge impact was my shift." – Laina Raveendran Greene

Humility and empathy enable you to identify better and more effective solutions for other people. Approaching problems with humility and empathy is deeply rewarding for your own life. By acknowledging your own limitations, and recognising that something is really difficult, you are giving yourself an opportunity to learn.

Think about how you approach problems in your own life. Do you say, "This is an opportunity to learn something new, and to build new relationships as I seek ways to address this?" Or do you say, "Oh no! I should be able to deal with this! I must work this out for myself, or people will think I'm an idiot! If I can't deal with this I'm a failure!"

The first approach, where you seek to learn, is a humble approach. You cannot ever fail when you approach a problem as an opportunity to learn. The second shows that your ego is in the driving seat— YOU "should" be able to deal with something; the fact you cannot means that in your mind, you have already failed.

"I enjoy watching Audrey and Laina develop Angels of Impact because they approach it with humility. Every problem is an opportunity to grow. For Audrey, when she realised that her first social enterprise, PlayMoolah, was not fulfilling her growing desire to bridge the gap between 'knowing' (how to deal with money) and 'doing' (actually using money better), she was not frustrated; instead she sought a new way to bridge that gap. And that led her to Angels of Impact." – Lizzy Hawkins

Humility helps us to recognise that, alone, we can never have a huge impact on the world. We are well acquainted with stories about individuals who have changed the lives of millions—Mohandas Gandhi, Martin Luther King, Nelson Mandela, and Rosa Parks. What we are not told—because it makes the telling more complicated—is the story about the thousands of people who supported them and made their work possible. The people who joined the protests, and made lunch for the people on strike, and even bailed them out or tended to their wounds. No one operates alone. Our power to change, as humans, is rooted in our relationships with others. Even the people we talked about in this chapter, like Bright Simons, Alfredo Moser and Muhammad Yunus, depended on networks of people to make the changes they sought.

We cannot expect to make a huge impact on the world, alone. That would be our ego talking. Rather, if we recognise that there are local heroes and local innovations that need our support, then we begin to channel our efforts to co-creating solutions instead of being a saviour.

What We Have Learnt

- The poor are not helpless victims and are no less hardworking than others. They may have made the choices they did because there were no better options.
- Put aside our own assumptions, practise humility and treat the poor as partners when working to address their problems.
- It is important to take the time to thoroughly understand the problems the poor face and to co-create solutions with the very people most affected by poverty.
- Solutions imposed from outside fail. Local innovation is best.
- Networks of people make change happen. Even the most influential figures in addressing poverty or injustice did not act alone.

CHAPTER 4

LIMITATION OF CHARITY

"Charity is a form of trickle-down economics; if the trickle stops, so does help for the needy" – Professor Muhammad Yunus[81]

How do you feel when you give money to charity? Are you content with your impact through donations? If not, why is that?

You are probably giving your money to organisations doing amazing work. They provide clean water, fund children's schooling, or stop people dying from diseases that can be treated for pennies. You probably receive regular updates from them on how your money has helped: $10 buying five mosquito nets, or $50 digging three wells, or $40 per month to feed, protect and educate a child.

So why do you feel so dissatisfied with your efforts, even though you are donating to such good causes? You may wonder, "Is it my ego? I know I can't save the world, but why can't I be satisfied?"

Now that you have come so far through the book, you may even be wondering if you are not being sufficiently humble—maybe, that is why you are frustrated.

We used to feel frustrated too. We found that the basic model of a charity is mostly donor-driven, and often exhaustingly limiting. It seemed like this model could never address the huge needs of half the world's population. And morally, it felt uncomfortable because it perpetuated our privilege by making us the benevolent donors and poor people the passive beneficiaries.

You may have started reading this book to better understand your faint, somewhat guilty discontent about giving to charity. In this chapter, we will unravel some reasons why the business model with charity as its source of revenue is so limiting, even if it is doing incredible work. Also, charity usually addresses the symptoms of the problem but seldom the systems causing the problem itself.

You can't make your money go further

One frustration of giving to traditional charities is that it feels very restricted. Your $10 only ever buys $10 of mosquito nets. Your $40 dollars per month will only be able to buy that one child $40 worth of help. It can feel very frustrating to keep giving and giving and make such a small difference—when what we want to do is transform people's lives. In most cases, charities are unable to multiply the impact of your dollar. A dollar remains a dollar.

'Bonsai non-profits'

At the moment, charities really struggle to expand their work. Expansion usually means investing in the organisation, employing more people, re-training existing staff and increasing spending on overheads like offices or transport. Donors do not like organisations that are not spending money directly on the people they are meant to help. So they give funding to charities that minimise their overheads. But this limits a charity's ability to grow and bring their work to more people. Employing an extra person could dramatically increase a charity's impact. But if it decreases the proportion of donations to the charity recipients, the charity has to make a choice between being more effective or keeping its donors.

Ramakrishna N K, who set up Rang-De, India's first crowdfunding platform for small entrepreneurs, explains that this approach creates 'bonsai non-profits'[82]—organisations funded project-by-project by donors, unable to invest in reaching out to more people. He gives striking statistics of two million non-profit organisations existing in India—one for every 600 people.[83]

Reliance on the goodwill of strangers

As well as feeling limited, you may feel that giving regular donations cannot be sustainable. These organisations rely on the ongoing goodwill of donors like you to keep giving money. They devote immense energy to raising money from donors on the other side of the world. You, the donor, may be thousands of miles away from the people being helped. You will never meet them. So what happens when you need money to deal with problems at home? You, regretfully, stop donating. It is an extremely precarious model for such important work. And there is never enough donor money to address all the problems.

Too much focus on reporting to donors, not long-term results

It can take a long time for a charity to recognise that their solution has not worked and to change their methods. This is because charities, however committed their workers, are not accountable to the communities they help. They are accountable to their donors. So if a charity's well breaks or becomes contaminated, a community will have to be lucky to have donors who care about long-term outcomes. Donors should want to know that wells remain in operation, that communities have been effectively and sustainably educated about hygiene, that there have been ongoing reductions in water-borne diseases and an increase in the number of days children are in school. The donors then need to insist on these outcomes and withdraw their money if they are not being achieved. But this is rare.

"A friend in Malaysia was trying to help a women's charity, HomeNet Indonesia, to raise money. HomeNet Indonesia helped women to develop livelihoods by working from home and selling products. The amount that HomeNet required for a particular project was relatively small and I

thought I could have a greater impact by donating my time, rather than just giving money alone. I donated money through the Rotary Club and another friend of mine came in to add to my contribution. So we were able to give $10,000. But when HomeNet reported back, they only described outputs like workshops and trips they'd organised for the women. I didn't see anything tangible. They had no idea whether their work was actually lifting women out of poverty or what the next steps should look like to keep this sustainable. I realised that the charity world is not results driven. Many NGOs go through the motions of doing things as they are used to reporting to the donors. And donors are willing to give on the basis of these reports." – Laina Raveendran Greene

It feels horrible being a charity case

The final disadvantage of the traditional charity model is that it can be self-perpetuating and demeaning. We are not saying that giving people free things makes them less likely to use their own resources to help themselves. That ugly argument has been used to justify any number of inhumanities. Moreover, there is no evidence that giving people free things makes them less likely to pay in the future. In fact, a rigorous study[84] of communities looked at whether families which received free mosquito nets were likely to buy a net subsequently, compared to families which had not received a net and families who had been asked to pay for their nets. The families that had received the free nets were actually more likely to buy a second net at full price. After having used the net and learning that their families would be healthier with its use, they recognised the net's value and were willing to pay for more.

So we are not saying that giving people things makes them helpless, or lazy, or less likely to help themselves. We are saying that when communities rely on support from outside, which does not involve them, they become vulnerable if the support is withdrawn. And on a personal level, receiving charity, however well-meant, is just not a very comfortable experience. It robs one of a sense of dignity.

We will explore loss of dignity at a personal level that you may be able to relate to.

"While a student, I went to see friends in a different town and was stranded in a bad neighbourhood late at night. I had taken the bus, by far the cheapest option as I was pretty low on funds. The bus arrived late at one end of the town and it would take another hour on a local bus to reach my friends' place. I'd checked the bus timetable and knew that I could connect with a local bus to cross the town, even at that late hour. So I waited. It was in the UK during winter, so it was chilly and a misty rain was falling. The local bus departure time came and went. And I got colder. No bus. After half an hour, it became clear that there would be no bus.

"So I called my friend, late on that cold, rainy night and my friend drove across town to pick me up. She didn't mind—in fact she told me off for waiting so long before calling her, as I shivered and dripped in the passenger seat of her car. She was happy to see me, happy to help. Was I happy? I'd been given what I needed—I had even saved money on the bus fare. I felt incredibly grateful to my generous friend, but I didn't feel happy. I kept apologising. I was cross that the bus had let me down and put me in the position where I had to get my friend to drive across town on a cold and rainy night." – Lizzy Hawkins

"My driver in Jakarta had borrowed some money from me to pay for his kids' school fees. When I was leaving, he still owed me. I said, 'That's alright, don't worry about the money.' And that hurt him. He would have preferred to feel that I owed him money because he had served me for two years loyally and deserved a bonus, and that bonus would have helped write off the debt. He did not want me to just write off the debt, he needed to feel he had worked it off. I realised that it was very insensitive of me, that I should have consciously said, 'Actually, I owe you this money for the work you've done and it comes to the same amount that you owe me.' Despite my cultural awareness and empathy, even I was very insensitive to his pride at that moment." – Laina Raveendran Greene

Think about a time when you have been in trouble and needed help. Maybe your car broke down and you called a friend for a lift. Or you could not pay your rent and borrowed from a family member; your friend, brother or cousin may have been happy to help, or they may have sighed and rolled their eyes and told you off for your predicament. We suspect that you were not full of joy to receive their charity.

Charity does have its limits on a national level. There is a huge amount of research and debate about 'aid dependency'.[85] Aid dependency is the idea that countries become reliant on foreign aid and do not develop their own industries and governance structures. Food aid is particularly criticised for this; countries that receive free food have no incentive to develop their own local food production. Then when the food aid is withdrawn, those countries are left without a local food industry because it could not compete against the food aid. So they have to start buying expensive food imports. Haiti is the best example of this. When it stopped receiving food aid, 80% of its grain stocks were bought from the US because its local production had been so stunted by years of cheap or free grain.[86]

This makes more sense when you think, "This could be me. What would I do in that situation?" If you lived in a poor community and saw money coming into your world from somewhere else, it would make sense to try and get your hands on some of it. So people try to work in the relatively well-funded charities and NGOs that receive foreign money, rather than starting businesses and developing the local economy. A country's textile industry can often be a good indicator of whether aid has stifled growth, because textile factories are often the first types of industry to start in developing countries and the first to suffer a loss. There are real-world examples of this happening on a countrywide basis; Zambia received a lot of aid and saw much lower growth in its apparel industry than Honduras, which received much less aid but was similar in many other ways.[87] Clothing donations can also harm a country's industrial development. A 2008 study found that used clothing donations to Africa were responsible for a 50 percent reduction in employment in that sector between 1981 and 2000 on the continent.[88]

The debate about the effect of aid on growth has raged for decades. Some argue that aid efforts fail because not enough money has been spent. Others claim that aid corrupts and weakens institutions. We are not here to arbitrate on that debate. But when we look away from big, countrywide perspectives, we know that on a personal level, people do not want to receive charity. We do not want to be pitied, or be 'charity cases'. We want to be productive and responsible. And if for some reason we are denied that, we are likely to become angry at the system that is holding us back. Or, worse, we may lose hope regarding change. It is the same around the world; people do not want pity; they want respect and dignity. When they do not have that, they want the system to change.

Having said that, we must be clear on something; there are times when people just need help. When there are wars, natural disasters or crises, it is right to give unconditional assistance; many committed organisations offer it, enduring horrors and hardships to do so.

When we are working with entrenched problems that have been around for a long time, the limitations of the charity model—reliance on a trickle of donors, one-to-one return on donations, focus on serving donors rather than communities and a lack of real feedback about whether their actions are working—combine to keep charities small and struggling to expand their impact.

"Among the things that prompted my move from PlayMoolah was my desire to alleviate poverty and to have a more direct and systematic impact. I, too, had been through the journey of helping an individual and then giving donations to charities because I was seeking greater impact. But the question became, 'How long and how often can you keep giving to charity? And what more systematic ways were there of exponentially arriving at this impact for a longer period of effectiveness and greater sustainability that could really warrant the time we spent?'" – Audrey Tan

That's why we are so excited about the potential of social enterprises (purpose-driven businesses, or impact-first businesses). Social enterprises are not dependent on charitable donations. They do not suffer from these limitations and continuously innovate to ensure they have sustainable business models. They make their own money, which means that they can make money go further, grow faster and change more people's lives quiker.

What We Have Learnt

- The charity model has many limitations.
- Depending on the donations and goodwill of people removed from the problem is a precarious way of solving the poor's problems.
- Charity only addresses the symptoms of the problem but rarely works to change the systems causing the problem in the first place.
- There is no dollar-multiplying effect in charity, it stunts the development of the charity and posits donors as benevolent benefactors and the poor as passive beneficiaries.
- Depending on charity long-term creates aid dependency and stunts the country's own industries and governance structures in addressing the problems of its poor.
- The social enterprise model holds great promise in better addressing poverty.

CHAPTER 5

SYSTEMIC CHANGE TO END POVERTY

"True compassion is more than flinging a coin to a beggar;
it comes to see that an edifice which produces beggars
needs restructuring." – Martin Luther King Jr.[89]

How do you view the people whom you want to help? Be honest with yourself. Is it possible to believe, really believe, that you could be in their position, if you had been born to different parents or had different life experiences?

Poverty is difficult to imagine; it can only be experienced.

"As a British woman who grew up in the UK, went to university, and never had to worry about where the next meal came from, it's difficult to look at a woman in a slum in Indonesia and imagine life in her shoes. I'd probably have grown up hungry and been sick, without the treatment I needed, and ended up with long-term pain or disability. I wouldn't have had a good education because their public schools are ill-equipped, so I might not have been able to read very well. I may have seen corruption as a natural part of life.

"What decisions would I make then, if that had been my life? What decisions would you make, if that had been your life? How would you raise your children? Would you care about sending them to school if school had done nothing for you? Would you feed them a balanced diet if you didn't know what one was? Would you tell them that they could achieve more than you had, if you never had any role models who had done so?" – Lizzy Hawkins

Empathy will help us to understand something fundamentally important: when people are in need, the system is usually at fault, not the people.

Think about William Kwamkamba who made the windmills, or the Barefoot College ladies who developed the solar stove. Give people the opportunity and they can be more inventive and determined than you or I. But when they grow up in a system which does not give them those opportunities, all that potential is wasted and they get trapped in a cycle of poverty.

Realising this can flip our entire perspective around and help us look for more effective fixes. We will (and must) stop asking how we can change these people to fit them into a system. We will start asking why the system is failing these people and what can be done to change the ineffectual system.

This chapter relates stories of people who decided to change systems, not address individual problems. You will see the difference between addressing a problem and changing a system.

Look at it this way, you might visit a village in which most people are involved in farming and have their own tiny businesses on the side. That is, indeed, the reality for the majority of the world's poorest people. They have hardly any money, so their children are hungry, sick and uneducated. You attempt to help, with a programme to sponsor the children's vaccinations, mosquito nets, shoes, schooling and decent meals.

But you never asked the parents why they cannot afford to educate their children. You forgot to ask, "What is wrong with this system that parents cannot provide for their children?" If you had, they might have said, "A local landowner took the land where our tap was located; we can't irrigate our fields, so we can't grow as much. If we had a new well we'd be able to grow more, the farmers with bigger farms would be able to hire more workers on their farm and the crops would be better. Then we'd all be able to sell more and earn more money. Do you think we want our children to be hungry and sick?" So rather than the ongoing cost of a child sponsorship programme, you could put that money and energy into improving the water supply—make an up-front investment in irrigation so that the parents can look after their own children.

"'Systems change' for me means that we can operate in new paradigms that allow people to be more in tune with one another. For instance, if we look at today's capitalist system, we know it works somewhat. Capitalism has served us well from an economic standpoint. However, we are confronted by some of its shortfalls, such as how goods are currently produced. Take for example, fast fashion. To support demand, things have to be produced very quickly; lost in this high demand, we don't see the impact of production on the lives of people who may be working in exploitative factories with bad living conditions. The system thrives often at the expense of people and lives. So in this new paradigm, people will be thinking, 'How can we put people first, as opposed to profits first?'" – Audrey Tan

"I never really thought about systemic change until I joined Ashoka, the global organisation that invests in leading social entrepreneurs. I already knew there was a difference between social enterprises that work on the ground versus those which just sell, buy and resell products (like middlemen), but I didn't know that there was a term for it. Ashoka is very clear about that, though. An Ashoka fellow is a fish swimming in the opposite direction; a person who has identified that something is broken and recognises that they have to move in a different direction from everyone else who is telling them, 'You're stupid, ours is the way the world works.' An Ashoka fellow works towards systemic change. Lynna Chandra had set up Rachel's House hospice in Jakarta, as there was no concept of palliative care in Indonesia. The prevailing attitude was, 'You're dying, so you're off the system.' Lynna was the lone fish moving in the opposite direction, in small ways, helping the dying children. She had created a huge ripple effect that led to governmental policy change. Now, she is helping to train hospitals in palliative care. By moving in a different direction, you lead everybody to change to a new direction. That's 'systems change'." – Laina Raveendran Greene

So in systems change, you identify something that is wrong in the system, you do something to change it, and keep doing it until it becomes mainstream.

In the introduction to this book, Angels of Impact identified that many impact investors do not want to focus on poverty because it is high-risk and offers low returns. We have also identified that investors tend to overlook women; yet women are the key agents in ending poverty, and are without access to the funding and resources to scale up their impact effectively. So the system is flawed in the way that it addresses poverty and women. Angels of Impact is working to change that thinking. Fortunately, the mainstream is slowly shifting to thinking that women are good investments. However, they are not doing enough about it; definitely not with women in emerging markets. When the mainstream thinks of funding women in emerging markets, they always think about micro-finance and not of larger amounts that the women need to scale their impact. We are trying to shift action in that direction—to focus on women as agents of change and as good investments for larger amounts. A key indicator for us would be that in five or ten years, our efforts would no longer be needed! Once we invest in eradicating poverty, it will cease to exist. Once we invest in women, we would not need a separate structure for women.

Also, to truly transform the lives of people living in poverty sustainably, we have to look at the bigger picture. What made people poor in the first place? Were they displaced by conflict to places where farming is difficult? Do they struggle to get good prices for their crops? Have they gradually fallen behind because there are no roads to where they live and no electricity, so they cannot compete with places that can use roads and electricity to bring better quality goods to market? Has a long-running drought eroded their savings? Has pollution from nearby sources contaminated their fields? Are they discriminated against so they cannot access education or healthcare, or challenge injustice in the courts? Did a big factory close down with no alternative employment in the area? Were their skills overtaken by technology that could produce the same goods more cheaply and quickly? Did they, or someone in their family, have health problems that went untreated and meant they could not work?

It can take time and patience, as well as humility and empathy, to really get the answers to these key questions. People are not always up-front or understand the real reasons behind their problems. They might be too proud to admit that there are any problems in the first place. Some may think that you are a rich person with money to spare (and to them, you would be), so they may only tell you what they think you want to hear to get your help. It is human nature!

You need to listen humbly, and patiently, and really try to understand what is happening. And always, always think, "This could have been me."

Once you have a sense of what is wrong with the system, you can start exploring opportunities to change it. It will be easier to understand 'systems change' by looking at a few examples. We begin with one of the main inspirations for starting Angels of Impact: a woman called Dinny Jusuf and her work in Toraja Melo.

Toraja Melo: creating a market for the weavers of Toraja

Dinny Jusuf married a man from Toraja, a remote region on the Indonesian island of Sulawesi. She noticed little children of mixed race running around the village and wondered what was going on.

Figure 9. Dinny Jusuf. Source: Photograph provided by Toraja Melo. Reprinted with permission.

Dinny realised that weaving had once been the only source of income for many of the villagers in these rural areas. Weavers were mainly women who were homebound and lived in extreme poverty. The weavers in the villages were incredibly skilled in the intricate art of back-strap weaving, creating a fabric called *tenun*. But weaving a piece of *tenun* takes time, planning and immense dexterity. Yet, their exquisite, complex weaving no longer gave them a means to survive. They could barely sell the odd piece to passing tourists, and the local villagers were no longer wearing *tenun*. So the women had no choice but to leave the village, with many moving overseas to become domestic helpers and some even sex workers. Sadly, more often than not, they returned pregnant, abused and traumatised. The little mixed children running around the village were the products of their hardships. Meanwhile, the art of *tenun* was also dying.

Dinny analysed the system, not the problem. She asked, "Why do these women have to go overseas to make a living in the first place? Why can't they make money from this beautiful weaving?" She did not ask, "How can I bring these women more money? From their jobs overseas?" or, "How can I stop these women being abused when they work overseas?" She asked what was wrong with the system that caused women to leave their village instead of making money from their incredible skill. That question was important.

Dinny learnt that the weavers were not connected to markets outside Toraja. They did not know what might sell in a wider market. Worse yet, even in Toraja, tourists and locals were being offered cheap, machine-made weaving from China or other parts of Indonesia which undercut the women weavers' *tenun*. The women could not even sell to tourists.

So Dinny set up Toraja Melo, and began to have fashion shows in Jakarta with *Head to Toe Designs*. She started selling high-quality bags, clothes and shoes through a boutique in Jakarta and an online store, which increased sales. Dinny and her team created fashionable designs incorporating the *tenun* for a unique touch and used the urban poor to create innovative products from the women's weavings. Soon, celebrities and diplomats—even President Barack Obama's sister—would order her clothes, and as the prestige of *tenun* grew, even the locals began wearing it again. To help ensure the weavers' access to raw materials that are cheaper in bulk, and ensure master weavers taught younger weavers, Dinny set up weavers' cooperatives to commission work and give the weavers a regular income.

The impact on the community has been huge. From earning nothing to possibly US$40 a month, the women now have a regular monthly income of US$150-$220. Now that they know that *tenun* is valuable, even their husbands are wearing it again and village leaders are promoting its use in festivities. The villagers have regained their pride and fewer women need to leave their villages anymore.

Figure 10. Dinny Jusuf with one of Toraja Melo's weavers. Source: Photograph provided by Toraja Melo. Reprinted with permission.

Dinny transformed the system that ruled the Toraja weavers' lives. She created value for a product that was previously considered worthless. She established a new market for them to trade in goods that they could not sell before. And she built a sustainable way for poor people to make a regular income. Most importantly, she gave the women of Toraja an opportunity to escape a cycle of poverty and violence.

A better-known example of 'systems change' to help the poor is Grameen Bank's development of 'microfinance'.

Grameen Bank: banking for the poor owned by the poor

Professor Muhammad Yunus had been working in rural Bangladesh on a project to create a farmers' irrigation cooperative. But in spite of the project's success, many families in the village of Jobra were still trapped in poverty. He asked, "What is wrong with the system that these people are still poor?" He learnt that they had no land, and that the families often supplemented inadequate income by growing crops, or producing handicrafts like baskets and footstools. But to do this, they needed to borrow money even for small amounts of seed or bamboo. Their only recourse were local loan sharks who charged high interest rates and insisted the women sell their wares back to them, at a price determined by the moneylender.

Professor Muhammad Yunus learnt that for merely borrowing US$27, the families became trapped in a cycle of debt and poverty. This was the same across forty-two families. He was struck that such a tiny amount could cause such hardship. But the banks had refused to serve the poor. Their argument was that the poor could not repay loans; they had no credit histories, no collateral, and being illiterate meant that they could not even fill out the bank's forms.

The system had effectively failed the families by not offering loans under reasonable lending conditions. If the poor had access to money they could buy more raw materials, make more goods, sell more and earn more money. So he set up Grameen Bank as a banking cooperative, offering 'micro-loans' to the poor in Bangladesh. It began with the forty-two borrowers from Jobra in 1976. By 2011, Grameen Bank had 8.3 million borrowers, 97% of whom were women.[90] Its loan repayment rate is 98% and—most importantly for Grameen Bank's aims—64% of borrowers who had been with the bank for five years or more were no longer trapped in the cycle of poverty.[91]

Professor Muhammad Yunus, like Dinny Jusuf, did not just want to solve one problem, but wanted to make the system work for the poor. He saw the talent and perseverance of the women in the villages he visited and knew that if the system could be shaped to work for them, they would do the rest. He was right.

We will return to the story of microfinance later in this book to examine how new, greedy players have entered the picture to tar it with an ugly brush.

Our final example of 'systems change' looks at a basic service that richer people take for granted—electricity.

SELCO: bringing electricity to the poor

Harish Hande had returned to India while doing fieldwork for his PhD in solar energy engineering from the University of Massachusetts. He saw endless villages without electricity. The day would stop at 6.30 in the evening when the sun went down, as families used smoky kerosene lamps and stoves to cook, often spending over five times the amount richer people, connected to the national electricity grid, paid. Already passionate about the potential of sustainable energy technology, Harish asked, "What is preventing these people from using sustainable energy sources?" Like Muhammad Yunus, Harish learnt that poor people were not seen as viable customers for technology. He encountered the same excuses: they could not afford it, they would not be able to maintain it because they were illiterate (and therefore stupid), they were suspicious of solar power and preferred to use kerosene, no company could make money selling to the poorest people in India, and so on and so forth.

Harish was not convinced. So he asked more questions. He learnt that the money people were spending on kerosene and candles was greater than the instalments to buy a solar lamp or install solar panels on their rooftops. He learnt that many people had to choose between using light for critical household chores or income-earning activity. He learnt that children were going to school but unable to study at night without light. He learnt that some villagers were suspicious of solar energy because they had been given, or bought, poor quality solar products that did not work after some time. Most of all, he learnt that once the people were convinced that his technology could work, they really wanted it. But they could not access it, as they were unable to afford the legally required down payment, did not have the collateral for loans and could not pay the interest rates.

So in 1995, Harish set up SELCO Solar Light Pvt Ltd to provide sustainable energy solutions to under-served communities.

He wanted to bust the myths that the poor could not afford or maintain sustainable technologies, and that a business focussed on the poorest could not work as a commercial venture.

SELCO ensured excellent after-sales service to overcome the negative perceptions arising from other dubious solar technology that the people had experienced. SELCO made sure that it listened to its customers' needs and designed its services around them. Most importantly, it worked with banks, cooperatives, micro-finance lenders and NGOs to formulate financing packages that the poor could afford—always ensuring that they pay no more than they would have paid for the kerosene and candles, which they no longer needed.

Throughout the years SELCO has served over 200,000 households and brought light to over half a million people.[92] This light extends people's productive time and enables them to earn more money, from stitching sarees to crafting bindis. It allows shop owners and street sellers to extend their hours and children to study longer. All because one man asked why the system was failing the poor and found ways to change it.

Now let's meet a man who has made it his life's work to listen to communities living in poverty and tackle the issues facing them from a systems level, thereby enabling them to help themselves. His trust in the wisdom of poor communities led to the creation of an entire parallel economy—with a surprising currency! He shared his groundbreaking perspective on poverty, charity and the ignored wisdom of the so-called 'poor' in an interview with us. See box story.

Understanding Anshu Gupta's Unusual Success

**Figure 11. Source: Goonj... a voice, an effort [Digital Image]. (n.d.).
Reprinted with permission from: http://goonj.org/page_id=22834/**

Anshu Gupta is a social entrepreneur and the founder of Goonj—a non-profit based in India. Goonj's innovation lies in recognising the value of discarded clothing and turning cloth into currency. It uses clothes and other used materials discarded by the rich inhabitants of India's cities to pay rural communities and enable them to solve their own problems. We were lucky enough to meet and interview Anshu about his views on charity, poverty and the ignored wisdom of the so-called poor. First impressions belie this soft-spoken, unassuming man's achievements, but his passion and determination quickly surface as he speaks about his work. It is no surprise that his efforts have been recognised as transformative by the World Bank, NASA, the Schwab Foundation and the World Economic Forum and that he has also received the prestigious Ramon Magsaysay Award in 2015.[93]

The idea of clothing—cloth—as currency may strike you as odd, but Anshu says that clothing is a basic human need that is not commonly discussed. To him, food, clothing and shelter are the basic needs we can all list; yet clothing does not feature among the hundreds of targets set by development organisations.

Anshu himself first realised the importance of clothing in 1992, while studying Mass Communication. As a budding journalist, he spent a week following a corpse collector, Habib, around the old Delhi area. Anshu was shocked to learn that in winter, Habib's workload increased so much that he could barely keep up—from four to five bodies a day in summer to ten to twelve in winter, all within a tiny area. Anshu saw bodies in thin cotton shirts; people had clearly died of cold. He wondered if people in Delhi could not get the clothing they needed to stay warm and alive, then how would the poor in the villages of India and the rest of the world cope.

Suddenly, the notion of cloth as currency is not so strange. If you give people cloth, they would not have to find the money to buy it; cloth equates to money.

Anshu quit his job and set up Goonj in 1999, with 67 pieces of personal clothing that he and his wife had collected. He aimed to enable communities to solve their own problems. Goonj's 'Cloth for Work' scheme paid people clothes for their labour and enabled communities to address village-level needs. Goonj started with small projects, cleaning a village or de-silting a pond. It later moved to bigger projects, digging wells and building bridges, but always using the 'Cloth for Work' model. It was important to Anshu to offer cloth and other collected materials as payment for labour, rather than as a form of charity. He states that, "Across the globe, the biggest asset of village communities is their self-respect—their dignity." Anshu fully intends to preserve that dignity.

Anshu is passionate about the need to respect and be led by the wisdom of the communities within which Goonj works. "There is something fundamentally wrong somewhere. There is a huge development sector at work; there are hundreds of UN agencies and big people and there are a lot of small institutions. And everyone is talking about public welfare. And if the thought process is so correct, if we are on the right track, then how come the poverty is there and why is it increasing? I think it is because we, the learned people, the so-called educated people, a very small number of people, decide on the agendas for the rest."

His experience on the ground has taught him the flaws of taking pre-packaged solutions to communities. "We (the development sector) are only working on the surface; we are not going deep; we are not understanding what is the root cause. You are absolutely happy to tackle certain problems of the migrants and the slum dwellers in the cities. But do you understand why these people are emigrating? If I talk about India and many other nations, one of the main reasons is water. Why do I say that? Because 70% of Indian lives depends on agriculture. You are either a farm owner or a farm labourer. When there is no water, agriculture does not happen. When agriculture does not happen, employment does not happen. When employment does not happen, you emigrate. When employment does not happen, even education does not happen. So we as a nation, or corporate CSR or whatever, are absolutely happy to support teachers in village schools in India. But why are you doing that when the students are not there? The students are not there because they have emigrated. So if in a 10-month education cycle, a student is not there for four to five months, what will be achieved in these schools?"

He accepts that it can seem negligent not to address issues that one feels are important, but that is dwarfed by the importance of respecting the situation in each individual community. "In many countries, including India, we are talking about toilets. Open defecation is a curse, and, yes, it needs to end; people need to have a toilet. But suppose that in the larger part of the country you do not have enough water to drink, and yet we make toilets. Every time you flush the toilet you need six to ten litres of water. How will that work, especially if I'm bringing water from 3km just to drink, and half the world is going through a severe shortage of water?"

"So what I'm saying is that we are not thinking in a loop. We just think of one part. We say, 'Okay, fine, this is how the problem will be solved.' If you go to the private schools, including across India, every third or fourth kid is wearing glasses. If you go to the so-called *poor people school*, from a municipality school to a village school, you see hardly any kids wearing glasses. So my question to the wider development world, the people working on development and education, is, 'Is education suffering because the teacher-student ratio is wrong and the education policies are wrong, or is it suffering because the kids cannot see?' How many of us have really invested our time and energy in finding the reason behind these so-called poor communities?"

"Likewise you realise that in Nepal, India, Bangladesh and many other parts of the world, you hardly ever see a truck driver wearing glasses. They deal with dust, heat and long working hours without proper lights on the roads at night. So my question to the world is, 'Are accidents happening because the roads are bad? Or are they also happening because the driver is unable to see?'"

The power of Goonj comes from its total respect for the knowledge of the local communities. "We are able to use even second-hand material as such a resourceful thing, to barter for such huge infrastructure changes, because we never go to the people and say that we know everything. In a remote village, how can you and I know how much water comes in the month of July? Only the villagers who live near that river will know. We assume that we already know their wisdom. Why? Because we are educated, and well-dressed, and speak English? The moment you start looking through their lenses, the options are totally different. Sitting here, we all can decide, 'Oh, Cambodia, Vietnam and India have very bad roads— we need to create roads.' And that's when you say, 'Right, here is $1 million, I'm the big agency, I will now work with smaller NGOs and we'll build roads.' How do you know that the people in this village are not saying, 'No, the road is fine. I can walk on the road. I don't have water. Can someone clean my pond?' I (the development sector) am looking at MY resources, and MY wisdom, and I'm deciding. How many projects or schemes in the world are there where the receiver is a part of the decision making process, in whatever way? How many times do we make the mistake of leaving them out of the thinking process? And that is the reason why a lot of these projects ultimately fail."

"I'll give you a small example. We're building a lot of wells, all across the country. There are a lot of government projects digging wells, which fail. In our case it doesn't fail. Why? We are not technicians. We are not engineers. We know nothing about water. But the village community knows exactly what to do because when the machines and the technology were not there, and the consultants were not there, the wells were there. In these few years or decades, they (the development sector) have really started neglecting the wisdom of the locals. We (Goonj) go to an area, and just find out from the villagers when the rain happens which channel the water flows through. Say for 10 months it's a dry village, and for two months the water happens and it forms a channel. If you dig a well somewhere in that channel where the water flows, the probability of capturing water is much more, because that's the usual path of the water. Every time it rains, water takes the same track. So instead of digging a well somewhere else, if I dig a well in that channel, I might find water at 10 feet or 20 feet, instead of a hundred feet. Common sense says that for one to two months, that channel is absorbing a lot of water."

Anshu puts his belief into practice. "We have been very open because we thought we have to learn, we must never go in thinking we know everything. So in 2008 in one village we started asking what work we can do. They said there was a big shortage of water there. There is only one hand pump, next to the river, so when the river overflows in the rainy season, that hand pump is not accessible. We asked, 'Is there a well available?' They said the government had dug one, but it didn't work. They couldn't find water. And we asked, 'Why?' One of the seniors in the village said, 'Because they didn't listen to us. We know the water is here.' And he showed us a place and said, 'That's where the water is, but they didn't listen to us.' The villagers have something they do with a coconut to find water and instead of finding a scientific reason for why it might work, the world just says, 'Nonsense!' They say it's useless faith. It was a new thing for us too and with our urban arrogance even we didn't want to believe it, but we said, 'Fine. Are you sure the water is there?' He was dead sure."

"That's when we decided to build the well there. And we knew we were taking a risk. 20-30 people's manpower, and it might not work. But we knew that if the well failed and the water did not work, this chap was actually taking a much bigger risk because the villagers would not let him stay in the village. Because of their trust in him, so many people were working. So he was putting a lot more at stake in comparison to us. That's the first reason we did it. The second is that if in his place my grandfather had told me the same thing, it would have been impossible for me to say, 'No, you don't know anything! You are an illiterate villager! I don't trust your wisdom!' If my grandfather had said the same thing, I would have dug the well, then and there. That's the relationship. So we dug the well, and we got the water. That was our first well. To be honest, until that time, even we didn't know that our idea had such a big potential that we could dig wells in the future."

Anshu's driving force is his recognition that the people with whom Goonj works, despite all their strength and wisdom, and through no fault of their own, are struggling to survive. It clearly makes him angry. "Child labour is not by choice at all. Anybody who says child labour is a choice is talking rubbish. It's always out of compulsion. All across. And a huge number of people do not want these issues to be sorted."

"One of the toughest days for me, when I actually cried—and people say I'm a tough man, but I cried—was when in one village I asked a little girl in Hindi, 'When do you play?' And she asked me, 'What is play all about? What do you mean by play?' It took me hours to absorb that. How can a little kid, whose language is play, ask you what you mean by play? She has no concept of it because from morning until evening, this child is a bonded labourer in the bangle industry. And I say we forced her to work. If we had paid fair wages to her parents, who are also employed there, why would this kid work? When big money is made, it's important for all of us to ask, 'How did these people make this money?' I'm not saying everyone is making money in an illegal or unethical way. But in some cases there is something fundamentally, absolutely wrong."

"My regret is how we are really ignoring the wisdom. In India—I speak more of India because it's where I've spent most of my time—and in many other countries, people say (of the poor having large families), 'No, no, no, they enjoy it, that's why they have so many kids.' So I tell them, 'When you are pregnant, you go to a hospital. You might have a caesarean. That poor lady goes through labour every nine months. Is her pain less? You get three months of maternity leave. She doesn't get even a day off. You get the best possible food. She does not even get a cup of tea after giving birth. And every second or third kid, she loses one. Is she responsible for that? Or are we responsible for that because we never created health facilities? So it's not a choice; it is a compulsion."

"A lot of people call Goonj a development organisation. I always raise an objection. Development happens between zero and ten. Zero means at least two meals a day, some primary education, two pieces of clothing. In the kind of communities in which we work, they live below zero—in the minus. And our entire life will be spent just bringing them up to zero—from minus to zero. You can claim that's development, but it's actually survival. So we are actually working to make sure that people survive. Where is the development?"

Anshu also has no patience with the idea that people who donate to charity are in some way virtuous. He says they are simply paying back what they have been given. "In India, we don't get material from outside; we get it internally. In many parts of India there are very wealthy people these days, who may donate, but how can you call yourself a donor? Take me, for example. I come from a middle class family. I went to the most prestigious institutions in Delhi for my higher education. In the 1990s, the fees were about INR2,000. That was good money at the time, but ideally it should have been more like INR50,000-100,000, because of the kind of the infrastructure we had, and the kind of facilities we had. I always wondered whether, if the fees had been INR50,000, would it have been possible for a family like ours to afford it? And the answer is no. So in a way this person talking to you is the biggest product of subsidy. I have really eaten up the subsidies. The rich people eat up the subsidies. The educated eat up the subsidies. So now it is up to me to decide whether I have taken it as my right, or I take it as a debt and say, 'I have to repay this loan.' The fact remains that by doing something good, by giving a thousand bucks to someone, what do we do? I repay. I absolutely repay. People need to understand that it's not pure charity when rich people give millions and millions of dollars of their money. Why? Because you really made good money! Because when you started university, the land was subsidised, and the building material, and you got a tax holiday while you studied—using taxpayers' money. So because you didn't pay tax, the villages didn't grow. So you grow, the richest possible people grow, on subsidies. The day we all pay the genuine wages to every single person who works for us, pay taxes, return loans and do not become defaulters, things will begin to change. How many of us can really grow to these levels? The time has come to question ourselves when we talk about poverty in the world."

"The fact remains that I was born in a good family by luck. Maybe the good karma of my parents, but I had no choice in it. At birth I had no control. It is important for me to understand that the fellow citizens of the world need to have at least the basics in life."

To Anshu, the notion of 'donating' old clothes is even less laudable. "Cloth is the smallest possible thing. Fine, if you give a thousand bucks, call that a donation. But second-hand clothing? You have already used it to the core, now you want to discard it and you're calling it a 'donation'. It is a discard! It is a burden on you and that's why you're giving it away. Stop using the word 'donation' for old materials. Rather, be thankful for the people who use your second-hand materials as they give them a new life; they value the hard-earned money you spent on your discards."

Goonj makes many objects with the discarded goods that it collects. Yet, Anshu will not have people thinking that they are 'supporting' the organisation when they buy Goonj items. "We've created about a hundred different products out of waste. We even weave using audiotapes from old cassettes and videotapes! But we are very clear—we don't create products for charity. That is very important because the moment the product is made for charity, even the producer will not give it the right attention for quality. It is all about getting the right quality and selling as value for money. So when someone tells us that they are buying a bag to support us, we say, 'Don't buy it then.' If the same product goes to H&M, you'll buy it for US$100. You can buy it in my store for US$20. We are supporting you! Why cheaper? It makes perfect business sense. Our infrastructure cost is not that high. Our advertising cost is not that high. So we can always sell for a few percentage points less than our competitors."

Developing something so unconventional as a new economy based on cloth has brought Anshu more than his fair share of criticism. His message is that you have to persevere to make your idea work. "I've always been a bit like this. I tell my team that if people see you as a sensible guy, they also need to understand that you are a nuisance. Because things can't be simple and plain and goody-goody. There are a lot of experts who say, 'Mr Gupta, your model is not sustainable.' I say, 'We have been sustaining it for the past 18 years. On what basis is it not sustainable? Because your bookish knowledge tells you that?' A practitioner says that it is sustainable and it is growing. And a theory guy says it is not sustainable. Who is right? The chances of a practitioner being correct are much higher. I feel we do all this for ourselves, not for others; it gives us happiness, satisfaction and peaceful sleep. We put in our own strategies, our hearts and souls, and it is often important to listen to yourself and the people with whom you work, instead of outside agencies. Tomorrow when it becomes successful, it will become a case study, and they will start to say, 'This is how this should happen.' But in the process, why do we try to kill innovative thoughts?"

"It's a beautiful thing; so many business schools call me to give lectures and so on, and I always oppose the idea of a business plan as a starting point. I say, 'Business planning and all kinds of planning are very important. It's not that we don't do it, but if at the idea level, you want to do something different —in either the profit or not-for-profit sector—and you're told that without a business plan, nothing will move, how many people can really afford to do that?' If you think about Muhammad Yunus or Bill Gates, do you think these guys really created a business plan when they started? It was just a passion. In Hindi we call it 'keeda', which actually means a little worm or insect that itches to grow, like a crazy passion or desire that you want to nurture. You had some faith in yourself and you wanted to test it out. If they had been sitting with some business plan that said, 'Oh dear, I need $25,000,' it would never have happened. No crazy idea has ever happened because of a business plan."

Anshu is keen to ensure that Goonj always remains humble as an organisation. When we asked him about the mistakes he made along the way, he laughed. "It cannot be that we do everything right. In an institution as big as Goonj, with so many people, we must have made hundreds of mistakes. Maybe that's why I don't remember—because the numbers must be huge! Who knows? Every day we must be making them. I'll tell you one story. We worked on the sanitary napkin issue. We were firm that this is not a women's issue; it is a human issue. And we told the field teams, 'Listen, all our meetings should have men in them also. Why do you talk to the women only when it's a human issue?' All of us agreed that it made sense. But then we realised that as soon as the men came into the meetings, the women did not talk. We failed miserably. So we said, 'Okay, we'll have all-women meetings.' Then we realised that the mother-in-law was sitting there, so the daughter-in-law wasn't speaking. The segmentation within the women meant that we again failed miserably. So we said we'd have two or three different meetings. And that's how it works. You have to change yourself."

It sounds counter-intuitive, but Anshu would actually be glad to see Goonj go out of business—on the basis that others up the ante on what they have started. "We are giving you permission to copy our ideas. That's the official statement. Whatever we've done, it's all yours. We'll be the happiest people to be out of the business if you guys can take care of it. If you replicate and copy what we did, you might improve it, because we did our work with limited wisdom. If you add yours, it might become bigger, maybe more efficient. Why not? Do it! And let us be out of the business."

"The next thing we're working on is India's very strong second-hand clothing market; there's a barter system where ladies go door-to-door collecting clothes and giving utensils and so on in exchange. We're actually studying that and strengthening that entire structure. People say it's direct competition to us. When it's organised and strengthened the material will stop coming to us. It's a huge risk. But the fact remains that here is an existing system in terms of second hand material. If you empower that system, if you make it more efficient, if you fill the gaps using what you've learnt in the past 18 years, you'll get hundreds, thousands more people employed, which we, as an institution, could never do. So in all of our work we say, 'Instead of creating new things, you need to work on the existing things.' Why do you go to a village and create a new school? With one-tenth of that money you can repair the existing one and make it functional. It's very sad to see how we really ignore the existing things and create new things, whether physical, mental, or economical."

> Ultimately, his is a message of hope. "We all have one life. Some people are making small films, or writing about me, and they come to me and say, 'Mr Gupta, you've made a lot of sacrifices.' I always calmly say to them, 'You see a sacrifice, I don't see that. Why? Because maybe for many not having two cars and a couple of houses, and maybe a holiday in Switzerland, is a sacrifice. But I consider myself very lucky and very blessed,' because I consider that very few people actually have dreams and even fewer people work on their dreams. And the most blessed people on earth are those who dream in the right direction. So I come from that fraternity of the blessed people—I have a dream, I'm able to work on it and it is in the right direction. It can never be fulfilled because every day it grows, but that's down to my own choice."

Toraja Melo, Grameen Bank, SELCO and Goonj show what can be unleashed when a broken system is changed to include people who were previously excluded. Toraja Melo gave the women weavers opportunities to make a proper income from their weaving, so they did not need to leave their villages. Grameen Bank provided poor communities a way of acquiring finances to run small businesses. SELCO brought clean affordable electricity to poor people. Goonj took a readily available material, cloth, and turned it into a form of currency for development. All of these are easily, almost naturally, available to richer people. **What these organisations have done is not charity.** They changed the system so that poor people have access to the same opportunities and tools that people in developed communities take for granted. Systems change is about addressing failures in the system that hold certain groups back from opportunities easily accessible by others. It is about saying, "This market is not being served; let's change that," rather than, "Oh, these poor helpless people! We must save them".

More people and organisations have started to question how they can change systems, rather than simply treating the problems caused by the wrongs in the system.

Many of these examples leverage on women as agents of change. Harish Hande, Muhammad Yunus and Dinny Jusuf all found that women were more likely to return to their communities and put their skills to use there. They were more likely to repay their loans and invest in their families. This proves that women are great investments.

Learning about the effect of systems change altered how the three of us viewed charity. We realised that, if systems were working properly, we would not need charity. The natural outcome of this humble approach is to question why we should be in a position of privilege over someone else. Instead of saying that some people 'don't deserve charity', we realised that we would not even need to be giving to charity if systems are fixed. We can end poverty through systems change than through band-aid efforts.

What Have We Learnt:

- When people are living in poverty, more often than not, the system is usually at fault, not them.
- If we aim to eradicate poverty, we need to look at the root causes and effectuate systems change, not just address individual problems.
- Systems change is about addressing failures in the system that hold certain groups back from opportunities easily accessible by others.
- If given opportunities, the poor can prove to be more inventive or determined than those in developed communities. Necessity is indeed the mother of invention.
- Women are the key agents of change and are good investments. They are more likely to return to their communities and put their skills to use there, repay loans and invest in their children.

CHAPTER 6

SOCIAL ENTERPRISES ARE BETTER ALTERNATIVES

"The brands which will thrive in the coming years... are the ones which have a purpose beyond profit."
– Richard Branson[94]

Social enterprises offer a totally new approach to business. They say, "People should not have to fit the needs of business. Business should fit the needs of people." They say, "We will not sacrifice our mission for profit." Most importantly, they say, "We will do this differently. Let's put people first. If we make money, that's great, because then we can grow. But let's make sure we're making lives better first." This is what all businesses should strive be in the first place—a mechanism for solving problems and improving lives.

A significant problem that social enterprises often face is that using business to improve lives is completely alien to the mainstream business world. We have become so used to a world where business decisions are solely profit-maximisation driven, and where the idea of profit being less important than a social mission is just… strange. This commonly held view causes all sorts of problems.

For now, just think—which world would you want to live in? One where profit comes first while our poorest and neediest fall through the gaps if profit cannot be made? Or one where businesses are driven by the need to reach and serve the poorest and neediest? Take a breath, close your eyes, and believe this is possible. We can have a world where businesses work for people. We truly can! But we have to throw away our preconceptions about how businesses should run and work together to craft the institutions that will allow these incredible social enterprises to achieve their missions and grow.

People admit that capitalism works and yet they also recognise that it does not. So what do we do? How do we improve the capitalist system? The Guardian quoted Richard Branson in 2012 saying that "Capitalism has lost its way, and financial growth should no longer be the main driving force behind big business."[95] In his interview with Spiegel Online in 2008, Nobel Peace Prize Laureate Muhammad Yunus stated that, "Capitalism has degenerated into a casino."[96] Social enterprise is a powerful improvement.

That is why we wrote this book. It is a roadmap to a better world.

"Before I started learning about social enterprises, I thought I knew how businesses were meant to work. I'd studied economics as part of my degree, and worked with hundreds of businesses, from huge multinationals to tiny ones in garages. Businesses were meant to be profit-making, and if people couldn't afford what they were selling, that was unavoidable. A shame— yes, but not business' problem. I thought it was the role of the government to help the people who couldn't afford what the businesses were selling. That seemed reasonable to me being from a wealthy country with wonderful and long-established systems to provide education, healthcare and welfare to everyone. And if, for whatever reason, the government wasn't getting the job done, then charity stepped in—well-meaning people scrabbling for whatever money they could get to make a difference." – Lizzy Hawkins

Social enterprises flip that kind of thinking on its head. They say, "Profit only? How dull. How limiting!" Social entrepreneurs say, "Look at all that's wrong with the world! Look at the things we can do! Look at how business fundamentals can be used to do more good!" They say, "How blind, to focus on only boring old profit when we can CHANGE THE THINGS THAT ARE WRONG and use profits to do more good!" They will not be deterred by having to break new ground or being the first to do something. They will not be discouraged by a banker who says they cannot succeed. They will not be stopped.

We have been privileged to meet many social entrepreneurs along our journey as we created this book. They all share this tremendous, joyous passion. However difficult their work is, they persevere, because they know they are changing lives. It is energising just being around them. That is partly why we wrote this book—for you, the reader, to find your life enriched by learning about and connecting with these amazing people.

Social enterprises combine the social impact of a charity with the market-driven approach of a business. They aim to be commercially viable while achieving a positive social impact. The revenue that the social enterprise earns, and the profit that it makes, will usually be reinvested into the company to enable it to grow. Growth enables it to change the lives of more and more people.

You might say that plenty of businesses claim to make the world a better place— renewable energy companies that reduce pollution, drugs companies that cure diseases, media companies that make people laugh, or gymnasiums that help people get healthy. But social enterprises make it their main mission and top priority to change systems that have broken down and are causing problems, so as to improve the world. Self-profit comes second, and profit is desirable in order for the business to grow and scale its impact. With conventional companies, self-profit for founders and shareholders comes first. If you cannot pay the gymnasium's membership, you cannot go in for the exercise you need to help you become healthy. If you cannot afford the drug, you cannot obtain it to cure your illness. If you cannot pay the energy bill, you do not get energy. These are 'profit-first' companies where the shareholders, not the beneficiaries, come first.

A social enterprise begins with its beneficiaries. It says, "These people haven't got something they need. What in the system is lacking that they can't get it? How can they get it?" The social enterprise might then identify the needs of its beneficiaries, for example, "These people need income," or "These people need healthcare," or "These people need electricity." Then the business is built around finding a viable way to get it to them and even co-creating solutions bottom-up with beneficiaries. For the example of SELCO—the people at the heart of the social enterprise become its customers and its salespeople. In others—like Toraja Melo—they become suppliers and employees.

SELCO, Toraja Melo and Grameen Bank are all social enterprises. They are making a real difference to the lives of some of the poorest people in the world, and they are devoted to doing this. Yet, they are set up to be functioning businesses at the same time. Their operating model enables them to cover the costs and hopefully make profit, which they can reinvest. SELCO charges its customers, but ensures that those rates do not exceed the cost of the fuel that they previously used to buy; it simultaneously develops new financing tools for the very poor to pay in instalments or get low-cost loans. Grameen Bank requires that its loans be repaid, and Toraja Melo requires that its weavers produce high-quality creations for which they are equitably paid.

The difference between social enterprise and charities

Social enterprises enable your money to go further as they focus on impact and sustainability. When Laina first encountered Toraja Melo, she and a friend invested in setting up a workshop for them to develop prototype products for Jakarta Fashion Week, which would help to create new revenue streams. Toraja Melo was thus able to offer a bigger range of attractive products at the event and generated more sales, allowing them to offset the cost of the investment.

In Chapter 4, we explained how charities have to choose between spending their income towards building their internal resources to help more people and spending that money directly on the people they are trying to help. Money spent on hiring a new nurse cannot be concurrently spent on vaccines for children.

A social enterprise model eliminates that dilemma; when money is spent, it does not disappear, but returns in the form of sales revenue, which can be spent again. SELCO is able to re-invest its profits into an innovation centre to improve the company's products, financial services and operations for greater efficiency and more tailored solutions to its customers' problems. A charity, on the other hand, would have to choose between funding an innovation centre and providing energy to the poor. On a social enterprise model, SELCO does not have to make that choice—it can do both as long as its business model is sustainable.

Charities are reliant on the goodwill of strangers to survive. Social enterprises are not. Social enterprises do not have donors; they have customers and investors. Social enterprises are not selling a sad story to someone thousands of miles away; they are selling quality products and services to someone that wants them and is willing to pay for them. That is a much more sustainable source of income than a well-meaning one-off humanitarian donation.

Having a commercial business model also means that social enterprises do not have another problem that charities face—not knowing (or in some cases, not caring) if their solutions are working. A social enterprise dealing with the impoverished as customers, not victims, learns very quickly if its solutions are right and if people are willing to pay for them, they're onto something; otherwise, they need to listen to their customers better and redesign their solution accordingly. Charities, on the other hand, are usually donor-driven and as long as the donor is happy and willing to contribute, the project continues. Some charities try to offer products and services but these are usually supplemental sources of income and they remain donor-dependent.

We have said that a charity model finds it difficult to expand its work because donors are focussed on projects and keeping overheads low. The advantage for a social enterprise is that it can be designed to scale up and up. Toraja Melo started with five weavers in Toraja in 2008. By 2016, they were working with over 1,000 weavers. That is a level of increase that a charity could only achieve with extremely huge donations. Toraja Melo achieved this by creating beautiful goods that people wanted to buy and were willing to pay for. Toraja Melo also entered into strong partnerships with a very scalable and sustainable social venture, PEKKA (an association of women as the head of their households), which also enabled it to grow quickly.

"Toraja Melo was able to remain focussed on its mission to provide markets and income to the weavers of Toraja. The weavers of Toraja were actively involved in the process of co-creating solutions that would sell. Dinny, the founder, spent a huge amount of time and effort with the weavers on

Toraja Melo's designs and colours, training them and making sure that they produced high-quality items and were committed to doing that. She had to ensure that the market liked what they were producing—and if something didn't sell, she and the weavers worked to redevelop it or create a new product. The weavers have never been passive recipients; they are an essential part of the business and Toraja Melo ensured that whatever was produced was of high quality that the market needed and was willing to pay for." – Laina Raveendran Greene

As you can see, the impact-first model adopted by social enterprises offers a more effective way to use money than the traditional donor model that most charities use. Social enterprises offer the opportunity to change the system to be financially sustainable and scalable to benefit more people. That is why we feel that buying from, and investing in, impact-first businesses is at the heart of ending poverty.

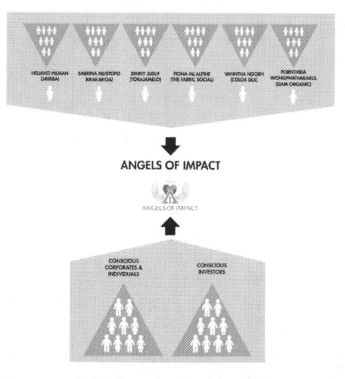

Figure 12

"Social entrepreneurs are not content just to give a fish or teach how to fish. They will not rest until they have revolutionized the fishing industry." – Bill Drayton, Founder & CEO, Ashoka[97]

Understanding social enterprise

Below are some remarkable real-life social enterprises, led by amazing women.

Empower Generation: women powering communities with clean energy

Anya Cherneff was working with women who were at risk of becoming sex trafficking slaves. She wanted to find jobs for them. Bennett Cohen was thinking about how to get people to start using green energy. When Anya and Bennett met Sita Adhikari in Nepal, the three of them realised that together they could not just help solve individual problems, but could create systems to improve the lives of women in Nepal. They decided to enable women to become clean energy entrepreneurs.

Empower Generation (EG) trains women, who live on less than US$2.50 a day, in basic business skills and technical knowledge about renewable energy products. It provides micro-financing to enable them to buy these products and become its local salespeople, offering EG's microfinance solutions for their customers to buy their products in easy-to-manage instalments.

So far EG has already enabled 20 women to set up businesses.[98] They, in turn, employ local women as sales agents, creating ongoing positive change—both for the women's income and the respect their community now gives them.

Not only that, EG's work has helped households in Nepal save US$2,040,473 on household energy expenses.[99] In a country where poor families typically spend 30% of their income on expensive kerosene for lighting and cooking[100], or where women can spend up to nine hours gathering firewood[101], that is a tremendous impact.

Finally—yes, there's more!—by using clean, renewable technology, families reduce their risk of respiratory diseases caused by unclean cooking fuel. This is a major issue; 4.3 million people die prematurely each year from diseases attributed to unclean cooking fuels—more than the number of people dying each year from malaria or tuberculosis.[102] The environmental impact does not end there. So far EG has prevented the emission of 12,224 tonnes of carbon dioxide that would have otherwise been generated from burning unclean fuel.[103]

The Fabric Social: jobs for women in conflict zones in Northeast India

After years of volunteer work in the international development sector, Fiona McAlpine was frustrated that, "all money-making endeavours were the domain of neoliberal jerks, and that the only noble pursuits in life involved elbow patches and empty bank accounts".[104] Fiona changed her mind about business after realising that the poverty-stricken communities with whom she was working in India's northeast regions were missing out on money from development agencies and NGOs. So, the 26 year-old Australian decided to start a social enterprise. The Fabric Social works with women in conflict communities in Northeast India, selling high-quality clothes from locally-grown, and made, Indian silk and cotton to Australian fashionistas.

Figure 13. Model wearing The Fabric Social garments with the women weavers. Source: Photograph provided by The Fabric Social. Reprinted with permission.

Decades of border conflict in the region meant that it was simply too politically sensitive for NGOs to work in those areas. Light-touch 'reconciliation' activity, such as counselling and therapy, was not helping the women get out of poverty. These women needed money, but when they tried to get jobs, all too often they were tricked into modern day slavery and human trafficking. Fiona had no money to give them, but she could give them jobs that utilised their existing skills.

She first worked with two villages that were already making cotton and silk. The Fabric Social team designed clothes of mixed silk and cotton and began to sell them in Australia. The company now employs weavers through a weavers' cooperative, and its entire supply chain is transparent and responsibly sourced—from the farms that feed the silk worms, to the weavers' cooperatives, to the fair treatment of tailors who construct the clothes. Perhaps the company's biggest impact is the fact that it has doubled its weavers' income since it was established in 2014.[105]

The Fabric Social brought systemic change; it created a market for products where one did not exist before and provided a new way for people in poverty to generate income. By working with the villages' women, The Fabric Social also shaped a social shift—the women have gained greater power in the community and are better able to influence decisions in their interests; not to mention, of course, the hope and dignity forged by being part of a successful business after years of conflict, death and suffering.

Figure 14. One of The Fabric Social's weavers. Source: Photograph provided by The Fabric Social. Reprinted with permission.

Javara: preserving Indonesia's biodiversity and indigenous culture

Helianti Hilman realised that indigenous agricultural practices went beyond the simple addition of fertilisers but that these practices were being lost. This prompted her to learn more about Indonesia's indigenous agriculture. She learnt that indigenous communities had become the guardians of Indonesia's biodiversity since the 1970s, while mainstream farmers began producing solely commercial strains of crops. The marginalised indigenous communities had stuck to their traditional methods and seeds, and were the last people using nearly extinct strains of crops. They lived in remote areas with little access to markets for their products and often in poverty. Meanwhile, mainstream farmers using commercial strains had to buy new seeds to replant their crops, and those expenses kept them in a cycle of poverty as well.

Figure 15. Helianti Hilman. Source: Photograph provided by Aditya Wardhana. Reprinted with permission.

Helianti saw an opportunity to improve the lives of indigenous farmers, while preserving Indonesia's biodiversity, and give the struggling mainstream farmers alternative farming options.

She created Javara to provide a market for these indigenous farmers' produce. Javara develops the produce into premium artisanal food and sells them in Indonesia's high-end stores and hotels. The company works with the farming communities to fill gaps in their knowledge of business and new farming techniques that could improve their productivity without compromising their traditional practices. Javara helps farmers acquire organic certification, and offers working capital to help them buy equipment.

Javara's ethos is about adding value to the farmers' high-quality produce. So, it develops novel premium products that combine different farmers' produce, such as coconut jam, flavoured salts and spice rubs. It offers quality assurance so that the products may penetrate premium international markets with strict requirements. It brands and markets the products to high-end buyers across the world, ensuring that the stories behind the products shine through. Exports to markets such as Japan, the US and Europe make up 85% of its revenue at present.

Javara currently works with over 50,000 farmers and 200 food artisans to sell over 700 products. It has had an amazing effect on the farming communities it works with and is an important player in preserving Indonesia's biodiversity. Like so many social enterprises, it is changing lives by giving marginalised people a market for their products.

As an added benefit, the indigenous crops may become valuable tools in adapting to climate change, serving as alternative strains in environments where commercial species fail. Such environments are likely to become far more common in the coming years.

Figure 16. Helianti Hilman connecting with the farmers.
Source: Photograph provided by Aditya Wardhana. Reprinted with permission.

Krakakoa: changing the face of Indonesia's chocolate industry

After spending six years as a consultant with McKinsey and travelling the world working on agricultural projects, Sabrina Mustopo came home to Indonesia with a mission. She wanted to fix Indonesia's chocolate sector.

She had seen first-hand how essential agriculture was to human survival. She had also noticed that the failures of the agriculture industry were driving migrants into overcrowded, filthy, disease-ridden slums in cities. "I realised that we can't have equitable economic growth if we don't touch agriculture. Why shouldn't farmers be paid as much as workers in Jakarta? They work hard, they're honest and they're skilled."[106]

She wanted to put more power in the hands of the farmers themselves. So she visited farming villages, offering training and equipment to enable the farmers to produce high-quality cocoa, which would command higher prices in the market.

Figure 17. Sabrina Mustopo (centre) with cocoa farmers.
Source: Photograph provided by Krakakoa. Reprinted with permission.

It took a lot of time and patience to build the trust of the farmers. "It's very foreign, this concept. 'Who is this person coming to this village and wanting to pay us more for cocoa beans, wanting to give us free equipment and training?' farmers were asking."[107] Time, patience, and a partnership with the World Wildlife Fund (WWF) in Lampung helped to make the change.

To ensure that the farmers received the most benefit from their new techniques, they needed a responsible buyer for their beans. That was where Krakakoa came in. Sabrina's company bought their beans for more than the Fairtrade minimum and created beautifully packaged, premium-quality chocolate bars. By buying direct from the farmers, they cut out the middleman and cut down costs to create a competitive product, which—all three of us, and many others, can attest to—tastes delicious.

Krakakoa now sells its range of chocolate bars through its own store and through six different high-end supermarkets in Indonesia. The company plans to grow further and improve more farmers' lives; it aims to work with 1,000 farmers by 2018. In the end, Sabrina wants to transform the way people look at agriculture. "I want families to say, 'I want my child to be a farmer.'"[108]

Figure 18. Woman farmer drying cocoa beans. Source: Photograph provided by Krakakoa. Reprinted with permission.

Color Silk: renewing lives in rural Cambodia

Color Silk is a social business founded by Vanntha Ngorn, a former weaver herself, in 2009. Vanntha had the opportunity to leave her village and get an education at a university, but during the aftermath of a financial crisis that affected the price of traditional Cambodian silk products, she was worried about the future of women in her village. Women were forced to flee to the neighbouring countries of Thailand, Vietnam and Indonesia to find a job, in turn causing them to be separated from their families and become vulnerable to dangerous situations such as human trafficking or harsh working conditions. Vanntha started Color Silk with the goal of providing Cambodian women a secure, safe and permanent job that still allowed them to be with their families. Color Silk helped to empower women through granting them financial autonoy.

Figure 19. Vanntha Ngorn. Source: Photograph provided by Color Silk. Reprinted with permission.

For those women who did not have prior weaving skills, Color Silk provided training that allowed them to start weaving basic products within 6 weeks. Once accepted as a member, Color Silk goes on to provide both financial and technical support to their members through providing them with loans to set up the looms and procure raw materials; and imparting them with basic design knowledge. Color Silk also seeks to ensure an all-year-round market that provides financial sustainability for their members.

Color Silk has 450 weavers as members of its community, and covers 6 villages in the southwestern province of Takeo. Members generate an average income of $65 per month, which is a 30% increase from their income before they joined the Color Silk Community. Color Silk supplies more than 50 boutiques in both Phnom Penh and Siem Reap, and provides 3 unique products of silk fabric, silk sarong and silk scarves to its customers. [All figures obtained from Color Silk's website[109]]

Figure 20. One of Color Silk's weavers. Source: Photograph provided by Color Silk. Reprinted with permission.

Color Silk has won a number of competitions and awards since its inception in 2009, including receiving a Starbucks *Share Planet Grant* in 2011 and participating in the 5th Global Forum on Innovation and Entrepreneurship in 2013 in South Africa organised by The World Bank's infoDev, a multi-donor programme that supports entrepreneurs in developing economies.[110]

Siam Organic: helping small-hold farmers move up the value chain

Pornthida Wongphatharakul and her co-founder Peetachai Dejkraisak, met in their MBA class. They were both troubled by the persistence of poverty among 17 million Thai farmers and failing government schemes for rice farming.[111] Upon graduation, they started to look deeper into the problem and designed a sustainable and scalable business model that could alleviate the problem.

Figure 21. Pornthida Wongphatharakul with the Jasberry rice produced by Siam Organic. Source: Photograph provided by Siam Organic. Reprinted with permission.

The business model includes providing pure organic rice seeds, organic fertilisers and farming input; training farmers on organic farming; exchanging best practices among the farmers; micro-financing; and offering a guaranteed market by purchasing all output.

Besides earning higher income from their produce, farmers also benefit from lowered production costs and increased yields. In addition, farmers are trained to grow certified organic Jasberry rice under international standards, ensuring that their products are of the safest and best quality.

Figure 22. Pornthida Wongphatharakul with Siam Organic farmers in their Jasberry rice fields. Source: Photograph provided by Siam Organic. Reprinted with permission.

Siam Organic is currently working with over 1,000 small-scale farmers who are achieving 14 times higher incomes compared to an average Thai rice farmer; the farmers' daily incomes have risen from USD 0.40 to USD 6.[112] Besides the increase in their income, health conditions of farmers and their families have improved, thanks to the nutritious Jasberry rice that they grow.[113]

Siam Organic participated in the *Spark the Fire* pitch competition in Silicon Valley in June 2016, held as part of the Global Entrepreneurship Summit hosted by President Barack Obama, and emerged top out of 80 start-ups.[114] They were also chosen as winners, out of 600 applicants, of the DBS-NUS Social Venture Challenge Asia held in Singapore in September 2016.[115]

As you can see, these amazing women social entrepreneurs are at the cutting edge of innovative solutions to sustainable poverty alleviation.

Having heard their amazing stories, we just want to warn you that not all social enterprises are created equal. The enthusiasm for 'inclusive business', while praiseworthy in many ways, should also set alarm bells ringing. **It is therefore important to note that good intentions are not enough. Additionally, just because a company sells to the poor does not mean they are "doing good". There are examples of social ventures that have also gone wrong or created harmful unintended consequences.**

"The road to hell is paved with good intentions." – Proverb

We found that the clarion call for inclusive business was C. K. Prahalad's 2004 book *Fortune at the Bottom of the Pyramid*. While sounding very honourable, it seems to have triggered a 'gold rush' to profit from the poor rather than benefiting the poor. A reliable source stated that Prahalad had originally planned to call his book *Fortune <u>for</u> the Bottom of the Pyramid*, but was persuaded by his publishers to change it to *Fortune at the Bottom of the Pyramid*.

The book argues that businesses should see the world's poorest—the BOP that we discussed in Chapter 2—as an untapped market worth up to US$13 trillion per year.[116] Companies that re-engineer themselves to deliver low-cost, low-margin, high-volume products and services for the BOP will get a slice of the US$13 trillion. The book gives examples of how companies which have done this have brought jobs, skills and money to remote communities, for example by partnering with local distributors and employing and training people from the community. Prahalad emphasises the need for companies to take a responsible approach to doing business with these communities, and applauds the fact that such selling methods to the BOP prevent the poorest people from having to pay more for their goods than richer people in better markets.

The business world seized upon the book's message, but many distilled it to just the title, thinking that there is a fortune waiting for companies who sell to the world's poorest. And by doing so, companies can claim to 'do well by doing good'.

Some big companies such as Unilever have shown earnings of US$6 billion per year from BOP markets.[117] It did this by reformulating its products, for example, creating single-use detergent sachets that are affordable to people who would struggle to pay for a large quantity at one go. It has developed an efficient infrastructure to deliver to the poorly-connected places where the world's poorest often live. It has tried, where possible, to integrate local logistics companies into its supply chain. This work is part of a wider corporate drive to improve health and reduce preventable diseases by providing low-cost soaps and other cleaning products to improve hygiene. Alongside sales, it offers education programmes to help consumers understand the principles of hygiene and instil habits like hand-washing.

In many ways, it has made a real impact on people and the environment by moving to responsible product sourcing and implementing programmes to improve health. But it is still a profit-first company. It sells its soaps, detergents and shampoos to make money, so it has a vested interest to promote the use of soap for hygiene. It would be useful to ask if there were any unintended consequences, for instance on local alternatives to soap that had existed before and may have been replaced by this sachet strategy? Were there local entrepreneurs who produced handmade soap who could not compete with these cheaper alternatives? These are some examples of questions that could be considered when trying to help poor communities to ensure there is more good than harm that is created when helping the poor.

Simply selling to the poor does not make one's business a social enterprise. Unlike conventional businessmen, social entrepreneurs are overjoyed when a rival appears. When Dinny Jusuf found that other buyers were competing for the textiles made in Toraja, she told us she was delighted. "I'm happy about it—before Toraja Melo started, nobody was wearing *tenun*, except for some ceremonial dancers. Now people are wearing it again and the local economy has grown as a result. Some people even say, 'Ha! You have created your own competitor!' because with more people buying from the weavers, the supply is not enough." Dinny turned things around for more benefit and rode the wave of *tenun*'s popularity by sourcing it from other regions; now Toraja Melo works with communities in Mamasa, West Sulawesi; and Adonara & Lembata islands in East Flores.

Here lies the difference between social enterprises and inclusive businesses. Social enterprises identify a social problem, formulate a business model to address it and persevere until the problem is solved. Inclusive businesses are focussed on profit-maximisation and will sell to the BOP only so as long as it makes good business sense, and will 'fight' to keep their market share and profit without considering if their products truly benefit the BOP.

We have other stories to help you understand why it is so important for businesses that serve the poorest people to focus on impact before profit. The first story is set in the microfinance industry and demonstrates what happened when profit-driven businesses used the microfinance model created by social enterprise to achieve their own profit motives instead. The other is about inclusive business and the hidden dangers unleashed by the new-found enthusiasm for selling to the poor.

When we discussed Grameen Bank earlier, we related how Professor Muhammad Yunus had proven that the poor would repay loans, flying in the face of the banks' claims that they would not. Grameen Bank's repayment rate of 98% is enviable—and astoundingly surprising to mainstream lenders who had vehemently doubted that the microfinance model could ever work sustainably. It did take Grameen Bank 17 years to be profitable, with sizable investments—estimated at US$78m—from governments and NGOs[118] to enable its growth and develop a worldwide microfinance industry, but it still remains a remarkable success.

When Grameen Bank reached profitability in the early 2000s[119] and proved that microfinance was a viable business model, the wider financial industry took a keen interest. New microfinance lenders sprang up, while existing ones were able to secure large new investments from commercial banks, believing that they would dramatically increase the number of people they could lift out of poverty. In 2006, there were 7.3 million active microfinance borrowers. By mid-2010, three of the biggest microfinance lenders were set to make millions of dollars by going public.[120]

Sadly, this was not about investing more money to transform countless lives. We wish that was their story, and we would have loved to tell it. But that did not happen.

The investors, and some of the newer companies, were only after financial returns for their investments—they wanted to see profits first. So the poor were pressured to borrow more, repay more, and take out multiple loans from different lenders. The carefully-tended peer groups and community stewardship that characterised the Grameen Bank type of lenders had disappeared, as aggressive microfinance agents were pressed to meet commercial lending targets. One loan officer, under pressure to report ever more loans, signed up 273 microfinance community groups in a month. Training protocols had prescribed that they should only form 12 groups in that timeframe—or 36 groups as an absolute maximum.[121]

The horrifying underside of this rapid growth came to light when borrowers started taking their own lives. In the Indian state of Andhra Pradesh, between 50 and 200 suicides were linked to aggressive microfinance companies. Terrible stories emerged. One woman drank pesticide and died the day after a loan agent told her to prostitute her daughters to pay off her debt; she had borrowed 150,000 rupees (US$3,000), but made only 600 rupees (US$12) a week. Another debt collector told a mother of four to drown herself in a pond if she wanted her loan waived—she did, the following day. An 18-year-old girl, pressured to hand over 150 rupees (US$3) meant for school examinations fees, also drank pesticide. Her suicide note said, "Work hard and earn money. Do not take loans."[122]

It is appalling! We are telling the story to underscore just how important it is for organisations working with the deeply impoverished to have a social mission at heart, and remain focussed on improving their lives. Once an enterprise is engrossed in delivering returns to distant bank shareholders, it ceases to be a social enterprise and becomes something quite dangerous.

Business can end up exploiting the poor. A business that is driven by profits first cannot concentrate on social impact goals. Some social enterprises find themselves moving away from their original customer base and instead start serving better-off customers in order to become more profitable. They then end up fitting in their social mission as a nice add-on to a profitable, profit-first business. They start looking more like for-profit companies that do CSR instead of social enterprises. We heard a story which may be a myth but offers a helpful example of how these processes can work: one Indonesian social enterprise was set up to help low-income women earn extra money; but once it received funds from an impact investor wanting to make profits and impact at the same time, the business model was changed to targeting male factory workers instead of low-income women. The company soon became more like a profit-first business helping a few low-income women as part of their CSR, rather than a social enterprise. That is why Harish Hande of SELCO has never succumbed to the temptation of doing lucrative solar installations, as he is very clear that his sole beneficiaries are the poor. He knows full well that if he diverts resources to serve the rich, he will not have the bandwidth to meet his targets to help the poor.

Our second story looks at the contrast when a social enterprise sells to the poor. We previously explored how SELCO and Empower Generation sell renewable energy products to villagers through a network of men and women whom they train. They clearly do not exploit these communities. Right from the start, both companies knew that their products should not make the poor worse off, so they investigated the communities to find out how much they spent on kerosene for lighting and cooking. These social enterprises knew that people who bought their products would no longer have to buy the smoky and harmful kerosene, so they set their price at the same level as the villagers' expenditure on kerosene every month. They also worked with existing banking institutions to set up microfinance instruments for their customers to take loans and buy their products in small instalments. SELCO even attracted investors to deposit funds into the banks as guarantees for the banks' loans to the poor.

They also gave serious consideration to after-sales service and support. Knowing that their salespeople and customers live in remote areas and would struggle to find replacement parts unless those were readily available, SELCO ensured that their salespeople knew how to maintain the products. It also developed products that use locally available materials as much as possible and ensured maintenance teams were within a reasonable radius of their customers' location for a quick and efficient response.

Thus, they used innovative financing and after-sales methods to keep both the cost of the original product and maintenance affordable.

Both companies focussed, first of all, on the wellbeing of their customers. As a result, they produced what their customers needed, at a price they could afford and with a payment system that worked for them. For SELCO in particular, their profits go into their innovation laboratory to develop more products and services that benefit the poor. Yes, they do aim to make profit. But unlike the profit-first microfinance companies, the ultimate goal of a social enterprise is to enable the poor, marginalised and vulnerable, and respect them as customers, suppliers, salespeople and employers. That is the opposite of profiting for self-enrichment at the expense of the poor.

The lesson of the microfinance tragedy is that when profit-first companies start selling to the world's poorest for the purpose of profit-maximisation, they can often do more harm than good.

What We Have Learnt

- Social enterprises offer a new approach to business and an alternative to charity. They combine the social impact of a charity with the market-driven approach of a business.
- A social enterprise begins with its beneficiaries. The ultimate goal of a social enterprise is to enable the poor, marginalised and vulnerable; and respect them as customers, suppliers, salespeople and employers.
- Unlike charities, social enterprises are not reliant on the goodwill of strangers to survive. Social enterprises do not rely on donors; they have customers and investors, which enables them to carry on with their work in a more sustainable manner.
- Just because a company sells to the poor does not mean they are "doing good". Social enterprises identify a social problem, formulate a business model to address it and persevere until the problem is solved; whereas inclusive businesses focussed on profit-maximisation will sell to consumers at the bottom of the pyramid so long as it makes good business sense.
- There have been examples of social ventures that have gone wrong or created harmful unintended consequences in some companies' rush to profit from, rather than benefit, the poor. Good intentions alone are not enough.

CHAPTER 7

THE PIONEER GAP

In recent years, the idea of social enterprise has taken hold and is growing rapidly. For example, in the UK there are around 70,000 social enterprises, contributing £24 billion to the economy and employing nearly a million people.[123] In the United States, it is estimated that the sector employs over 10 million people, with revenues of US$500 billion—about 3.5 percent of total US GDP.[124] Beyond that, numbers are hard to come by, particularly in developing countries where the social enterprise model is arguably the most powerful tool for social change. Bill Drayton, founder of Ashoka, estimated in 2006 that the citizen sector (another term for social entrepreneurs) is halving the gap between its productivity level and that of profit-first business every 10 to 12 years.[125]

Not surprisingly, another phenomenon that has happened is the rise of impact investors. Impact investors are investors who are attracted by social enterprises and aim to achieve positive social impact while still making money from their investments. Some impact investors ensure that the companies in which they invest meet certain social and environmental standards; others focus on particular sectors and invest in companies that have high potential to

95

make big changes. So an impact investor might focus on healthcare and invest in a new model of health insurance or a medical technology company that will improve healthcare while making money.

In their rush for the 'fortune at the bottom of the pyramid', many impact investors while professing to want to help the poor, get excited about a model that allows them to get rich while doing good. What could be better? Well, it is just not that simple. To put it bluntly, when you put social enterprises, especially those focussed on poverty alleviation through the narrow, old-fashioned lens of 'profit-first' businesses, they are actually not as attractive as they are made out to be. This chapter explains why that is so, how it is affecting social enterprises, and takes a first look at what you can do to help them grow and do more good.

In 2010, impact investors believed that inclusive businesses could reap profits of up to US$667 billion over ten years for investors[126]. In 2011, 52 impact investment funds (out of around 200 in existence at the time) planned to deploy US$3.8 billion within a year.[127] Considering that the world's 29 richest countries spent US$135 billion on development aid in 2013,[128] it was incredible for the private sector to be planning that level of investment in social impact businesses.

Then the story started to change. The investors could not find companies lucrative enough for them to invest in. Even Acumen fund, the impact investment fund with the lowest expectations of financial return, examined over 5,000 companies in ten years and invested in only 65—less than 1.3%.[129] Another 2009-10 study in Sub-Saharan Africa looked at 439 promising inclusive businesses, however only 32% were commercially viable and had potential to grow significantly. Of those, only 13% had successfully scaled up in reality.[130]

Many impact investors quickly concluded that social enterprises are a nice idea, but not viable in practice. We disagree. If a profit-first investment model does not work for social enterprises, we need a new investment model to gauge them by, especially when dealing with social issues such as poverty. We need to change the way we understand the core purpose of business.

Here is a vision to inspire you. In his book, *Creating a World Without Poverty*, Professor Muhammad Yunus envisages a world where social businesses compete in the same marketplace as for-profit businesses because the media and investors pay as much attention to a company's social impact as to its financial performance. He shows us a glimpse of what the world could be—if enough people commit to it—and presents possible versions of press releases in a world where social impact matters more than profit. We have reproduced some of them here:

> *"DHAKA, BANGLADESH: The CEO of People's Sanitation, a social business devoted to providing high-quality sewer services, water treatment facilities, and environmentally friendly garbage disposal in urban areas throughout South Asia, announced the results of a new study showing that rates of infectious disease have fallen by 30 percent in the cities served by the company. Shares of People's Sanitation rose from 12.00 to 14.50 on the London Social Stock Market as a result…"*

> *"NEW YORK: At today's annual investors meeting of Health Care for All, a social business that provides affordable health insurance for poor people in the United States, a new board of directors and executive vice president were elected by dissatisfied investors. 'Over the last year, we've seen some progress toward achieving our goal of providing health insurance for every poor American,' the spokesperson of the major investors said. 'But we think we can do better in the coming year. The new leadership we've selected today will help us reach that goal…'"*

> *"TOKYO, JAPAN: Executives from two of the world's leading social businesses, Global Water Supply, based in Tokyo, and Agricultural Irrigation Industries, headquartered in Seoul, Korea, today announced plans to merge their organisations. Observers say the merger will produce greater efficiency and assist both companies in pursuing their mission of providing pure water at low cost to poor families and farmers in sixty countries of the developing world. Investors appear to agree, as shares of both companies rose on the Tokyo Social Exchange by over 30 percent in the wake of today's announcement…"*
> *pp.180-181*[131]

Keep this vision in your mind as you read this chapter. We will explain how social enterprises tackling poverty do not fit easily into the traditional, profit-first focus that drives investors and why most of these social enterprises will not make as much money as profit-first companies. If any of it makes you feel that social enterprises cannot survive in the current system, think of ways we can all play a part in making it real. We can have a world where social enterprises thrive and are supported to achieve their world-changing goals.

First, let us examine why it is far harder for social enterprises focussed on poverty alleviation to make a lot of profit than it is for profit-first companies. The title of this chapter, 'the pioneer gap', is a phrase coined by the Monitor Institute in a ground-breaking 2012 report, *From Blueprint to Scale*, which examined the barriers for social enterprises focussed on poverty. Social enterprises have to be pioneers in several areas: they have to pioneer logistics to reach the world's poorest communities, they have to pioneer business models that make money while achieving their mission, and they have to pioneer education among their target groups to win trust. They often work in areas where the cost of doing business is very high, which explains why traditional businesses are not already there. Yet, all the while, impact investors are only looking at the bottom line without understanding the context within which these businesses operate. Impact investors gauge social enterprises against businesses that work in areas where infrastructure exists and the cost of doing business is lower.

Social enterprises working with the world's poorest also pay the 'Bottom of the Pyramid Penalty'

It is difficult running a start-up company in general. Most budding entrepreneurs end up in debt, living hand-to-mouth and juggling creditors like circus clowns. It is said that one in three new businesses fails in the first three years, and if you succeed, it still takes time to move from just surviving to paying yourself a decent salary or even just breaking even.

Now consider this—most profit-first companies:

- are dealing with customers who can read their marketing material;
- have access to the Internet and a reliable power supply to keep it working;

- have access to bank accounts and credit cards which can tide them over the times when their cash flow gets tight;
- have customers who, in turn, have bank accounts and credit cards;
- can hire and pay skilled staff;
- are able to set up a store or an office in a place that customers can reach by driving down well-maintained roads or public transport;
- have a relatively reliable supply base;
- are able to distribute their products through established logistics networks;
- can access existing market research about their customer base so they can target their sales and avoid wasting money trying to reach people who won't buy their products; and
- operate within clear regulations to protect consumer rights and business interests.

Infrastructure. Financial systems. Education. Legal protection. Even with all of these available, we know how hard it is to ensure the success of a regular start-up.

Imagine now a social enterprise which wants to change the lives of the poorest people, who have access to few, or none, of those advantages. The social enterprise is dealing with power cuts; slow or non-existent Internet connections; uneducated customers and staff; lack of distribution networks; roads that range from potholed to non-existent; and customers whose extreme poverty makes them extraordinarily cautious about the smallest purchase, particularly because they have no faith in the legal system for protection or justice. This social enterprise's customers are hard to reach and have extremely limited resources. Its suppliers are small-scale, scattered and often unable to provide consistent supplies.

The 'BOP Penalty', as we explained about earlier, is the extra cost that the very poorest must pay to receive basic services that richer people take for granted. It is the extra cost of getting goods to markets along dirt roads that are full of potholes or completely washed-out. The higher prices of those goods, once transported at great cost to remote areas where the poorest live, are also transferred to a social enterprise working on poverty alleviation.

The BOP Penalty exists in the first place because profit-first businesses, or even governments, have found it expensive to operate in these areas, and therefore there is either no service or costly service. It costs too much to bring goods and services to populations that are unable to pay the expense of overcoming the barriers. Why would any company pay millions of dollars to build a good road to communities that will never be able to buy enough products to cover the cost of the road? Why pay millions to extend the power grid to reach people who cannot afford what the richer people, who are already on the grid, pay for electricity? This is why expensive public amenities like roads, electricity networks and broadband networks have typically been built or backed by governments. In countries where the government's resources are limited, these are only provided for those who can pay enough to eventually cover the cost.

Social enterprises that are trying to reach these communities and lift them out of poverty, do things that make no sense to conventional profit-first businesses or even governments. SELCO could make far more money if they used their painstakingly-developed, low-cost business model to reach wealthier consumers at a higher margin. Toraja Melo could massively boost profits—or lower their prices—if they employed weavers in a factory in the cities where their goods are put together. But they have resisted that temptation and stayed true to their mission.

This, fundamentally, is why social enterprises focussed on poverty alleviation are unable to live up to impact investors' unreasonable expectations. Amidst the hype around 'inclusive business' and the 'fortune at the bottom of the pyramid', one important fact got lost—if there was a lot of money to be made in improving the lives of the poor, wouldn't profit-first companies have been there already?

That is also why we consider social entrepreneurs as amazing, passionate heroes or angels. They have to be. Anyone who is not passionate, committed and driven to overcome obstacles, day after day, does not remain a social entrepreneur for long.

"The last time I spoke to Dinny Jusuf, she was visiting Singapore and we were on a bus. 'Sorry,' she said to me, as she replied to a message on her phone. Then, 'Ah, I'm so sorry,' as, seconds later, she checked her phone again and wrote another reply. After the third time, she stuffed her phone deep into her bag and said, 'I just have to stop looking. I'm not there; there

isn't really anything I can do.' Earlier, I'd watched her talk to a group of social entrepreneurs about Toraja Melo, in her typically passionate and sometimes hilarious style. But now, she almost broke down. 'Oh, I'm going to start to cry,' she said. 'We've been working day and night for days and I'm so tired!' She explained that the company had finally won two big orders. Both customers were really good long-term prospects; the orders were big and the company had agreed to a tight turnaround time to get the orders. Two of Toraja Melo's seamstresses—twins, both widows—had been working through the night to complete the order. But the electricity at their house, two hours from the Indonesian capital, Jakarta, had just failed that very day. 'They've been crying,' she said. 'I've been trying to make them feel better but they're so upset. They know how important this order is and now they don't know what to do.' She showed me a picture of the women's house: a dirt road stretched to infinity from the front step; there was nothing but trees and fields on the horizon." – Lizzy Hawkins

Dinny manages a fragmented and remote supplier base that stretches across thousands of miles and five different islands, along steep mountain roads that only motorbikes can travel on, and where electricity is so scarce and expensive that the beeping of empty government-installed electricity meters has become as common in the village as chickens clucking or dogs barking.

Dinny's life could be so much easier. She could employ weavers in Jakarta or Bandung, where electricity supply is reliable and transportation relatively easy (compared to an eight-hour journey to Toraja—though few would describe Jakarta's traffic as 'easy').

Dinny does not take the easy route because Toraja Melo is not about profit-maximization. It is about ending a cycle of poverty and violence that has trapped too many women for too long. Dinny will not put up with that. When she watches Toraja Melo having the impact she has worked so hard for, she feels enthused, gratified, validated and vindicated.

"Oh, you'll love this! This is great! We were talking to them about the impact of Toraja Melo on their lives—we do it to everyone, to understand our impact—and do you know what they told me? They said, 'Working with Toraja Melo doesn't make us rich, but we can plan our lives now.'

It made me so happy that they said that. It doesn't sound like much, but it means so much! They can make a down-payment on a motorbike, they can pay for electricity—they can budget for the future. It made me feel so good." – Dinny Jusuf, Founder, Toraja Melo

Social enterprises are not doing things that make profit-first sense. They are doing something far more important than that.

Social enterprises must pioneer new ways of doing business— they are the true innovators

On top of the difficulties presented by operating in remote, poor and needy areas, social enterprises must come up with new ways of doing business that do not fit traditional models. Social enterprises cannot solve their problems in the same way that profit-first companies do, because that would often mean compromising their mission. A company set up to bring incomes to remote communities by buying their goods cannot easily consolidate its supply base. If it tries to cut logistics costs by buying from a bigger or less remote supplier, it cuts out the remote communities it set out to serve; and if a social enterprise closes down completely, it has failed in its mission and left the communities it served in the lurch.

Social enterprises need to do things differently, which often means challenging commonly-held assumptions. The microfinance industry was born because a maverick like Professor Muhammad Yunus put his money where his mouth was to challenge the banks' assumptions about poor people's credit worthiness.

Social enterprises have to be pioneers. SELCO had to establish a whole new line of finance to enable its customers to pay for their products in manageable instalments. Toraja Melo had to set up weavers' cooperatives to enable its model to work. Empower Generation set up different finance tools for its sales agents and its customers to meet their non-typical needs.

This is another significant reason that impact investors have shied away from social enterprises that are tackling poverty. A company that is pioneering a new approach, especially in the high-risk, low margin world of extremely poor people, is a nerve-wracking prospect for an investor. As 19th century American industrialist Andrew Carnegie said, "Pioneering don't pay."[132]

The 2012 report by the Monitor Group on impact investing, *From Blueprint to Scale*, showed the financial penalties that these pioneering businesses pay. Acumen Fund—the impact investment fund that invests in inclusive businesses (which include, but are not limited to, social enterprises)—reported that its portfolio companies' average profit after tax is **minus** 20%.[133] That is not attractive. Acumen's eight *most* profitable investees record an average profit of just 6% after tax.[134] Acumen Fund is very selective about which companies it funds—it only invested in 1.3% of the companies it considered funding.[135] Acumen also works closely with those companies. Even then, it expects a return of just over 1x its invested capital.[136] In other words, it is just about getting its money back plus its patient capital. That is pretty off-putting to mainstream investors looking to do good socially and do well financially.

Social entrepreneurs must win over their target groups

People in poor and marginalised communities are accustomed to being exploited or ignored. So it can take plenty of time and energy to overcome their suspicion and persuade them that a social enterprise will genuinely help to improve their lives. Building trust can take years. Even when an entrepreneur is offering an obviously good deal, they have to overcome resistance. Sabrina Mustopo, founder of Krakakoa, recounts how she and her mother would visit villages in Java and offer the local farmers equipment and training to grow high-quality cocoa. "They'd just look at me like I was mad. Who is this woman, coming here and offering us equipment and training? Why would someone do that? What's the catch?"[137]

Similarly, Helianti Hilman, founder of Javara, wanted to offer a great opportunity to the indigenous farmers of Indonesia. However, it took a lot of time and hard work to overcome their resistance. They had suffered decades of exploitation from outsiders coming into their communities, buying up their land and treating them appallingly. Helianti needed to persuade them that she was different. In the end, she worked with a group of rice farmers near her parents' home in Central Java to help them market their products. It was only after she persuaded Indonesia's high-end supermarket, Ranch Market, to stock the products, that other premium retailers started ordering the products.[138] Finally, Helianti was able to convince the farmers of her serious and sincere intentions to help them.

The process of building trust is essential and time-consuming. And while it is in progress, it is very hard to make any money. Dinny Jusuf reported that when Toraja Melo began, "We'd buy all the weaving, regardless of quality—because it takes so long to make them and we not only wanted to encourage the existing weavers to weave for us, but also encourage other women to learn." Today, the company has a good pool of trained weavers and craftspeople to meet its high quality standards, but it has been a long road getting there.

On top of these challenges, social entrepreneurs may need to introduce something completely new to a community or—more difficult still—re-introduce something that has failed before. SELCO has been there and done that; it needed to persuade villagers in India that solar power was a better option than the dirty expensive kerosene fuel they had used all their lives.

How would you react to solar power if you had not learnt any science, did not have access to magazines or television that introduced the idea and had never heard of 'climate change'? If someone came to your home selling a contraption they claimed could use light from the sun to light it up at night, what would you think? If you would let the person into your house in the first place, he would give you a demonstration. Even if the product seemed to work, you would still be suspicious, "What if it's a con, and there's actually a hidden battery which will eventually run out and leave the contraption useless?" you might say to yourself. Or worse still, what if you had previously tried a cheap solar lamp that did not work, would you be willing to try a better solar option?

So a social enterprise trying to sell a new solution to poor communities must overcome mistrust born of decades—even centuries—of marginalisation, exploitation and ignorance, and persuade poorly-educated communities of the benefits of their solutions, that they are in their best interest and not that of the social enterprise. The next biggest barrier is to persuade them to spend their time or money on that solution.

This can be very staggering: when you live on less than US$2 a day, every purchase or time spent on something could be a matter of survival. In Chapter 1, we discussed the BOP Penalty and how that makes the poor reluctant to spend money for future gain. The poor are incredibly conservative consumers. They plan for the worst-case scenario because that is what often happens. Remember the farmers who refused to use all the fertiliser for the crops, as they expected a big flood to wash it all away? Or the weavers who said that working with Toraja Melo had not made them rich, but having a stable income has enabled them to finally start planning for the future? The very poor usually do not plan for a future since that is as unstable as their past. So any purchase that promises an improvement to their lives is offering something that they may not conceive of as possible.

These were all the barriers that SELCO had to overcome, and more— unscrupulous salespeople had already been to many villages with outlandish claims about the sun powering lights and cookers; and had sold cheap products, which were defective and expensive to fix. When SELCO's salespeople came around, the villagers would fetch their broken lights and recall the last time someone had tried to convince them that solar power would solve their problems.

At the bottom of the pyramid, quality control gets difficult. Copycats can fake good products, take the money and run. The poorest people are most vulnerable to exploitation because they are less able to confirm whether they are being offered a legitimate product, and when they are being conned, they are tragically seldom in a position to seek justice.

So when a social enterprise is offering a new solution—whether it is solar power, or insecticide-treated mosquito nets, or chlorine to purify water and prevent sickness—it needs to work even harder to educate these communities and persuade them to trust it. And the answer to, "How long does it take to educate a village?" is far less certain than, "How long does it take to build a factory?" A company pitching an idea that hinges on selling an unknown product to a suspicious customer base with no money is unlikely to face very good reception from investors.

Many impact investors are not investing in poverty alleviation

We have seen all the reasons that social enterprises focussed on poverty alleviation are unlikely to be as profitable as profit-first companies who do not operate in areas where the cost of business is high. For impact investors, the key metric is still profit. It makes sense because their investment model requires them to cover their costs and make profits. If they were to invest in potentially loss-making businesses, they would have to close shop in no time. Therefore, these investors tend not to invest in impact-first companies working on poverty; they are stuck in a system where they struggle to focus on impact ahead of profit.

The danger is that when investors claim to be impact investors, there appears to be sufficient funding for all social enterprises. In reality, the investments only go to social enterprises that are able to make impact and profit at the same time. Therefore, little funding is flowing to social enterprises focussed on poverty, which are facing a huge funding gap, despite the millions of dollars sitting in impact funds.

According to Oskar Haq, Asia Regional Financial Sector Advisor of Oxfam GB – Jakarta, "Due to the pressure of attracting capital, 'impact investing' as an asset class may be running the risk of losing focus on its primary mission and having an increasing bias to the 'demand side', meeting the needs of the investment community exclusively. For impact investment to achieve its potential for poverty reduction, it is critical that the attention of investors is re-focussed back to the needs of the enterprises themselves. Oxfam and Sumerian Partners have recently collaborated on a discussion paper titled, *Impact Investing: Who Are We Serving*, looking at the mismatch between supply and demand in the impact investment space" (Oskar Haq, personal communication, April 24, 2017).

David Soukhasing, a Frenchman living in Jakarta, is an investor. He manages an angel impact fund called ANGIN (Angel Investment Network Indonesia). He has worked in the investment world for most of his professional life.

"I was talking to David because I knew he had left one of the region's biggest impact investment companies, LGT Venture Philanthropy. I wanted to know more about that." – Lizzy Hawkins

See the box story for what David had to say.

Impact Investing Reality Check

"When I joined, LGTVP was an innovator and was pioneering things. It was very private equity-minded, but it decided to invest in the impact ecosystem by establishing an accelerator programme. I wanted to do that; it allowed us to both do investments and help companies. LGTVP was among only a handful of impact investors to use a mix of investment instruments—including debt, equity and grants. It was pretty innovative and exciting, and allowed us to look at different companies and take different approaches. It was much more like an impact-first approach; we looked at companies that impact investors wouldn't look at because they didn't offer the return on investment.

"Then the Managing Director left and the new management got a lot more conservative. Their attitude became 'Venture Philanthropy is fine, but we still want our capital back.' They were tired of capacity-building and wanted to go back to direct investment. We went from being established as a foundation to being a regular investment fund. We had to drop the debt investment and grant investment side, which had given us so much more flexibility. That was when I left.

"I've been disappointed by the [impact investing] space because I see these people who think you can get a high impact and high return. You can't expect both of them because it's not going to happen, at least not immediately. Impact investors are not philanthropists; they are very seldom motivated by philanthropy. They invest in capacity-building to create a pipeline or build their brand. Then they realise it's costly and seek the higher return on investment. I've seen a lot of impact investors get involved in capacity-building in the short-term, organising conferences and setting up accelerators and incubators, but I don't see them sticking to that long-term.

"It's the same with venture capitalists—I see them launching lots of accelerators, but only until they can harvest good companies."

When asked why investors claim to be impact investors, instead of normal investors, David responded, "I don't really know. Maybe companies think impact funds are more likely to get money from the IFC (International Finance Corporation), ADB (Asian Development Bank) or the World Bank? At the beginning, people investing in impact funds thought that they were going to impact and get a return on their money. When the performance of the fund is very poor, they get stuck in companies they will never exit."

Now David manages an angel investment fund in Indonesia, and his investors are keen to look at impact-first companies. A large part of his job, however, is still managing their expectations of impact—because they, like the other impact investors, still believe that getting rich and doing good is immediately possible.

"We look at impact because our investors are asking for impact. But then they face the reality on the ground. It's so hard to find companies that will earn a return. As soon as an investor gets stuck in a social enterprise and it doesn't move as fast as predicted, the investor will never invest again. Earning a return on the regular companies is already hard. When you add in a layer of impact and needing to survive from a business point of view, it gets harder."

In David's view, managing investors' expectations is an essential part of true impact investing. "You need people with decent expectations of return. People have to know what they're getting into. Don't expect the next Facebook to come out of a company doing handicrafts in South Sulawesi. We have turned down investors because their expectations are too high."

David feels that another element is being more creative about how to give returns to investors. "For example, you can look at the businesses and see if there's a way to get the return to investors not in terms of exit but in dividends. You choose slower growth, but with sustainability and profitability, so there's a dividend to be paid. There will be some return, but it's not going to hit two digits. Or after two years, you start harvesting a revenue share so you get part of the cash flow, revenue or profitability. So you might take 0.5% after two years and then get more if the company does well. If it doesn't do well, 0.5% doesn't hurt too much. If it does perform well, then you get a bit more."

If an impact-first business cannot offer the right level of return, David's advice is to focus on building strong business foundations prior to generating impact. "Focus on becoming operationally stronger, then focus on impact. So, for example, one company reinvested its profits into delivering its services, like training farmers and providing equipment, which slowed growth. It might have been better to delay support to the farmers and focus on investing in the company. If those profits had been reinvested into the company to improve its operational capacity, it might have grown faster, later. Some of the companies we invest in, we know won't make a big impact to begin with, but at a later stage they will have greater impact. I'd like to see them focus on building strong foundations first and then on generating impact."

Ultimately, even David has to think profit-first. Even with a mandate to seek companies that offer higher impact for lower financial returns, he constantly struggles to make a case for social enterprises that focus on the world's poorest. "When you look at BOP, they are hard to make a business case for, because it's hard to charge a market rate, they're more expensive to reach, more expensive to convert, more expensive to retain, and the lifetime benefit is lower. If you want to make a return you'd better target other people."

Our conversation with David backed up what the numbers suggested, and what social entrepreneurs have been telling us: impact investors are still focussed on profit before and above impact. This is bad news for social enterprises trying to bring solutions to the world's poorest people.

But David also surfaced possible solutions to the financing issues faced by social enterprises. First, expectations are key. People supporting social enterprises who serve the BOP have to understand what they are getting into. They have to be committed to generating impact over profit. That will help to avoid the issue that so many enthusiastic impact investors run into: they expect too much, do not understand that seeking impact may not always generate huge financial returns, and are ultimately disappointed. Another way to address the social enterprises' pioneer gap is for people to be creative in their support for these enterprises. High-interest loans hurt social enterprises and equity can too often drag social enterprises away from their mission. Experimenting with different methods of payment, providing in-kind support and helping to generate additional business are all ways that social enterprises can be helped.

The bottom-line is this: investors that only look at the financial figures of a social enterprise are completely missing the point. Social enterprises are changing lives, transforming whole communities, and bringing dignity and hope to millions. What these companies achieve make the slickest world-dominating high return technology company look extremely dull.

It is deeply frustrating to see social enterprises missing out on funding because of the conventional narrow worldview of investments for profit-maximisation. Even if we were to throw compassion aside for a moment, surely the pure economic value of enabling the poor, the marginalised, and the vulnerable to make as much of their talents and creativity as any of us, is immense. There are still many impact investing funds talking about the ability to do good socially and do well profitably, but when you examine their portfolio clearly, you see that they are not really investing in impact, or the impact has been compromised in the pursuit of profit. If we do not stop the hype that perpetuates wrong expectations, which lead to disappointment, we will never be able to find sufficient funding for social enterprises working to alleviate poverty in a systemic way. Some foundations, government development funds and even family funds are beginning to look at impact investing as an alternative to their traditional form of investing in charities. However, many unfortunately are also attracted by the "do well and do good" mantra of many impact investors, so funds are not flowing to social enterprises tackling poverty as the should.

What We Have Learnt

- Most impact investors have misunderstood investing in social enterprises as 'doing good' while generating similar high returns as normal businesses. Most were left disappointed when this did not materialise and subsequently pulled their money out of such funds.
- Social enterprises tackling poverty do not fit easily into the traditional, profit-maximisation focus that drives investors. We need a new investment model to gauge them by and change the way we understand the core purpose of business.
- Possible solutions for directing impact investors' flow of funds to social enterprises can include managing their expectations, garnering their commitment for the social enterprise to generate impact over profit and being creative with their support for social enterprise such as experimenting with different methods of payment.
- Social enterprises focused on poverty alleviation face a 'pioneer gap'. They often have to pioneer logistics, business models and education to accomplish their goals. A company that is pioneering a new approach, especially in the high-risk, low margin world of extremely poor people, will often end up paying a financial penalty.

CONCLUSION

You can make a difference!

"Never doubt that a small group of thoughtful, committed citizens can change the world; indeed, it's the only thing that ever has." – Margaret Mead, Anthropologist[139]

So what can we do? That's where you come in. How can you help bring about a world where purpose-driven companies can thrive? We promised you simple, practical acts that will help you share the joy of a life lived with purpose. We will talk about them now.

It is important to remember that the things you do every day affect the world in a profound way. You matter, tremendously. By being conscious of this, we can all live our lives in a way that makes the world better.

"A lot of our money is invested in a very opaque manner. When we put our money in an investment account, we don't know how the banks use it. We don't know what projects they're investing in. It could be oil, it could be palm oil, it could be digging up a coral reef to get more minerals—there's complete opacity. So the question then is how to use your money in a way that really works for the good of humanity, in a very concrete way that

113

is actionable. That solidified my jump to Angels of Impact because my question was, 'How do we take action around our money?' And I think also the fact that I went down personally to see the supply chain of Toraja Melo in Toraja, and meeting the women weavers was a very emotionally gripping experience. When you've seen that, it demands a response from you as an individual. And the question is that now that you've heard about it, what will you do?" – Audrey Tan

Put simply, we are suggesting a range of things you can do:

- Buy consciously.
- Make others conscious.
- Influence what your employer buys.
- Share your knowledge and networks.
- Invest responsibly and patiently.

Shop consciously

> *"Small acts, when multiplied by millions of people, can transform the world." – Howard Zinn*[140]

Every dollar we spend is a vote for the world we want. That is a heavy burden to bear—particularly, if we do not know anything about the companies we are buying from. They may be paying their workers poorly, employing children or ignoring hazards that can harm their staff. They may be polluting the environment, destroying ecosystems or squeezing their suppliers until they can barely survive.

And you are giving them money and power to continue doing these unconscionable things when you buy their products and services. Your lack of inquiry as to how the product came to you is silent approval of these unethical practices.

The first thing you can do to live a more rewarding life is to shop consciously. For affluent people, shopping has become a form of recreation. We buy something as a novelty; we are pleased with it, we wear it, eat it or watch it, listen to it or play with it—then it becomes just another thing.

It is far more enriching to buy something that has made people's lives better on its way to you.

Small acts can create a transformative ripple effect. For example, every individual can consume responsibly and reduce waste. And by consuming ethically, the money goes to a supply chain where people are not exploited. It is a small step, but its impact can be tremendous. And it is more enriching buying from a social enterprise, where you can see the impact you make. Having a sense of our interdependence in this world makes us realise the urgent need to shift what we do.

Now that you understand your role in perpetuating poverty when you do not act as a conscious consumer, how can you shift your consumption and shop with a conscience?

Here are some options:

- Learn more about the supply chain of the companies you usually purchase goods and services from, and look for better alternatives if you find that they make profits by perpetuating the cycle of poverty.
- At the end of this book is a list of the social enterprises that we have featured, with their websites, so you can gain a better understanding of what they do and find out how you may be able to support them (e.g. through purchasing their products).
- Learn about your local quality standards. The Fairtrade mark is recognised globally to signify that a product has been made with the best interests of its producers in mind.
- Learn about your local social enterprises and how you can purchase their products or services. Google 'social enterprises near me' and you may be surprised by what you find.

Last but not least, you can also tap into the Angels of Impact community that we are building. Visit www.angelsofimpact.com to learn more.

Make others conscious: the ripple effect

Our actions have a ripple effect. If you buy consciously, you are helping a community, but if you tell others about these wonderful products and the inspiring companies behind them, others will be moved to buy from them too. This will bring even more benefit to the social enterprise.

Laina and Audrey have put the ripple effect in motion. Laina wanted to support Toraja Melo's work and started sharing their stories with others. Because Laina shared her enthusiasm and joy for Toraja Melo's remarkable work and their products, many others joined in and started buying their products. Imagine the effect on other social enterprises if we all did the same. By increasing their revenue, you increase their impact.

There is no doubt that with the resources we have in Singapore, there is room for more resources to flow and have a larger impact throughout the region. Take Wiwid and the Indiegogo campaign (as mentioned by Audrey in her introduction) as an example. She needed $3,000 to go to school and we had the money within three weeks. Our friends in Singapore and Indonesia were able to channel their financial resources to her. They changed her life, with that simple act.

The ripple effect was a core reason for creating the Angels of Impact community; our individual wealth could only go so far, but we have had a far more exponential impact by unlocking the wealth in our networks. We are building a community to enable each individual's small contribution to add up to something huge. We are so grateful for the first pool of angels who have committed to joining our movement.

This ripple effect brings joy to not just the social enterprises, but also to those involved in flowing resources to them. So it is time to share this joy. It is natural to feel a little shy when you first start telling people about social enterprises that you support. But in no time, you will think nothing of it. And you will be incredibly moved to learn how many of your friends and colleagues are excited about what you have to tell them. They will want to know more and soon they will be spreading the word too! We have been pleasantly surprised by the number of people who are excited that just by deciding how and where to shop, they can make a difference. And we have been overjoyed by the enthusiasm and support we have received since starting Angels of Impact. People want to help and we have opened up avenues for them to do just that.

Influence what your company buys: go beyond CSR and include social enterprises in your value chain

Sometimes when we tell people who work in profit-first businesses about the work that social enterprises do, they seem slightly ashamed that their company is not a social enterprise. Many have told us that they have even thought about quitting their jobs to do something more meaningful. We say to them, "Stay where you are—you can still do so much good there!"

We find that corporations are enthusiastic about supporting social enterprises when given a chance. When we tell them what we are doing, they ask how they can help.

For example, Laina introduced Toraja Melo through her network of friends to high-end Jakarta furniture boutique, Arbor & Troy. Together, the two companies co-created a range of furnishings called the 'Conscious Collection', using Toraja Melo's textiles. This enabled Toraja Melo to go up the value chain and Arbor & Troy in turn were able to help Toraja Melo in their mission to revive weaving in Indonesia and help the poor earn a living. A true win-win!

Another way of helping is to have conscious corporates include social enterprises in their supply chain (shared value contracts). At the time of writing, Angels of Impact has already made sales of high quality products from our supported social enterprises to The National University of Singapore Overseas Colleges, Facebook, Twitter and LinkedIn as conscious corporates. We also work with procurement companies such as Compass Group (Singapore) who have championed us into organisations such as Bloomberg and Google procuring social enterprises' food products for their employee pantries. Through Audrey and Laina's links to Singapore's social enterprise incubator, raiSE, Angels of Impact also brought Toraja Melo's goods to Singapore's busiest shopping district through a store called Naiise. We hope to continue to secure recurrent income for these social enterprises through shared value contracts, so as to give the people living in poverty a stable income and a way to get out of this vicious cycle. You can help do the same for other social enterprises or help those within our community.

So think about what you can do in your workplace. Here are some ideas:

- If you are in a senior role, could you partner with a social enterprise to co-create products and services as part of a shared value partnership?
- Do you give out corporate gifts? Can you have some made by a social enterprise? You will not only get great products with a wonderful story behind them, they will also be a great boost for your employer's brand.
- Could your company change its suppliers to start buying from a social enterprise? Maybe you could try a catering company run by a social enterprise, or buy Fairtrade tea and coffee instead of those from other sources.
- Hold a tasting session of social enterprises' products at a work community event, or raffle a product made by a social enterprise to help open new markets for them.
- Join the Angels of Impact community and get ideas on how this can be done.

Share your networks and knowledge

When you start looking for ways to support purpose-driven companies, you will find opportunities everywhere.

Other than finance and new markets, the biggest challenge facing social enterprises is employing talent. They are always looking for people with the skills and knowledge that can help them. And they will need even more people as the social enterprise grows.

So a social enterprise might need your skills more than your money. Are you an accountant, or a social media expert, writer, web designer or skilled administrator and do you have time to volunteer? Believe us—your skills can be incredibly valuable!

If you do not know what a social enterprise really needs—ask! Social entrepreneurs and their teams have only one thing in common—passion for what they do. Beyond that, they come from all sorts of backgrounds and have diverse needs. They might need someone who can sort out their business processes, or revamp their website, or introduce them to potential clients in a certain sector—the list is endless, and you may be able to help. Or—going back to the point about sharing the joy—you may know someone who may be able to help.

The point is that once the community gets going, it can have incredible reach and impact.

Fund responsibly

As you saw in the previous chapter, social enterprises need finances to grow, and currently they are struggling in this regard.

Consider this—when you invest in a social enterprise, you enable that social enterprise to grow and transform lives. When you give funds to a social enterprise, you might get part of it back—or even all of it and more, depending on what the social enterprise needs at the time. This means that your money can be recycled; it enables a social enterprise to grow and transform many lives, and once repaid, it can be used to fund other social enterprises. You can give once and that gift can keep on giving.

Giving in a way to help a social enterprise grow has been called 'enterprise philanthropy' by the Monitor Group's 2012 report. As the name suggests, it is a cross between investment and charitable giving (expected to be returned with or without interest, although this is not guaranteed). It is about accepting a lower financial return because you recognise the difficulty of operating in areas where the poor live, but you know you will also get a huge social return with your money. Enterprise philanthropy will help social enterprises working on poverty overcome the pioneer gap and change the world for the better.

Now you might be thinking, "But I'm not an investor. I don't know any social enterprises. And I wouldn't know where to start." Look around and join other efforts that have been started, or start one.

You can take an example from Laina and Audrey, who have mobilised their networks for Angels of Impact. They have had moments of inspiration when they realised that they could double, or triple, the funding they could offer if they used their networks. Laina found a friend to match her donation to HomeNet, and later to Toraja Melo. Audrey asked her mother to match the money she gave to Toraja Melo. Thus, Angels of Impact is based on this idea of flowing resources around networks, to get the resources to where they will do most good.

"We are very fortunate to live in a world where technology, the Internet and social media can make those people-based networks develop a lot faster. But fundamentally, successful networks are about trust and authenticity. My cause has been consistent—I've been working on women's issues since 1997. So when I approach people in my network about something, they know, 'This is not about Laina getting richer, this is not about Laina's ego, this is about a cause.' And when you build that trust with people, then you move at the speed of light.

"Audrey, Lizzy and I have our integrity and our networks, and when we go to them, they know exactly where we're coming from. Angels of Impact has worked very fast, because the networks that we've built know us. The people who've signed up to be our Guardian Angels (core investors) know we would not do anything or say anything that they would not want to be associated with, so they have signed up with us. I think that's the power of trust—once you have it, you can move really fast. Then social media and the Internet make it move even faster." – Laina Raveendran Greene

The Internet has enabled us to make huge strides in opening up the world of investment. That makes us believe that a new kind of capitalism is possible because finally, the people who want to invest their money responsibly are able to connect with the right companies and also invest with others. In the past, investment was a closed world, confined to the professionals who measured companies purely by the profit they would bring. That model still exists—and dominates at the moment. But there is a powerful alternative, which we have the opportunity to leverage thanks to the Internet.

Another alternative is called crowdfunding. This is where individuals invest directly in projects and organisations they are passionate about. Crowdfunding has made it possible for people like us to join together in support of work that will make the world better. We do not have to be rich. Audrey knows a 16 year-old who earmarks 10% of her allowance money to donate to Kiva, the international crowdfunding site that offers microfinance loans to small entrepreneurs. If a 16 year-old can do it, so can we.

Crowdfunding has had an incredible impact since becoming popular in the last few years. Individuals can now learn about projects, charities and organisations, which are doing things they care about, and give money directly to them. It is a tremendous enabler. Crowdfunding allows us to bypass the investment managers who—because it is their job—are only interested in financial returns for their clients. Crowdfunding gives transparency to where the money goes and how it is used. The success of crowdfunding has seen millions of people prove that there are more important things than increasing the money in their own pockets. In 2012, more than one million crowdfunding campaigns raised over US$2.7 billion across the world.[141] There are regulatory barriers that are limiting the growth of crowdfunding in Asia, but it is still growing nevertheless.

So instead of giving your money only to charity, why not invest some of it in social enterprises? Your impact will be greater, and you will be able to get some, or all of your money back after a certain period of time.

Angels of Impact draws on crowdfunding to support its social enterprises. We have created a community of like-minded 'Angels'—enterprise philanthropists, social enterprises and corporations to channel our resources for exponential impact. We call it 'trust funding' as it is all done within a trusted membership network. If you think 'enterprise philanthropist' is too grand a title, do not be intimidated! Some of our early Angels included Audrey's mum and some of Laina's best friends. 'Enterprise philanthropist' is another word for 'someone who wants to use their money to make a better world through social enterprises'—someone just like you and me.

As you can see, there are so many things you can do. Do not underestimate the power of communities to help you do it. The process of forming Angels of Impact has strengthened all three of us in our determination to use our money and resources wisely, to help make a better world. The more you learn about the horrors of poverty and the uplifting work of social enterprises to end it, the more you will want to use your privileges to support these incredible organisations.

GLOSSARY

Bottom of the Pyramid (BOP) Penalty – *a phenomenon that sees the very poor paying more for the same goods than others, and making decisions with less access to information for the right choices.*

Business arms of charities – *profit-first businesses established to generate revenue for charitable activities.*

Charity/ non-profit – *organisations that rely on donations to achieve positive social change.*

Corporate Social Responsibility (CSR) – *a responsibility taken on by profit-first businesses to try to reduce the harm that they bring to the world and enhance the positive effects that they have.*

Creating shared value – *an approach that embraces social good as part of a company's core business strategies; the products they create inherently do good as they have clear economic, societal and/or environmental benefits and does resemble social enterprises but it is not.*

Crowdfunding – *raising money from a very large number of people, mainly carried out through the Internet.*

Enterprise philanthropy – *a financial strategy that prioritises social impact over financial return and funding into social enterprises instead of charities to maximise impact and sustainability.*

Impact investing – *a financial strategy that aims to achieve positive social impact while still making money from investments.*

Inclusive businesses – *companies that aim to include the world's poorest people in their business structures and processes, either as customers, employees and suppliers.*

Micro businesses – *fundamentally smaller than small and medium enterprises. They are also usually run by people who have no other options, sometimes also known as "entrepreneurs by necessity".*

Pioneer gap – *gap between the finance needs of social enterprises and the available finance, which arises because social enterprises are pioneering new and challenging markets, business models, and products and services.*

Social business – *a particular type of social enterprise that focusses primarily on the poor. Professor Muhammad Yunus who first came up with the term 'social business' has seven criteria he uses to define a social business. These are: 1) a social business' objectives will be to overcome poverty, or one or more problems (such as education, health, technology access, and environment) which threaten people and society; not profit-maximisation, 2) financial and economic sustainability, 3) investors get back their investment amount only. No dividend is given beyond investment money, 4) when investment amount is paid back, company profit stays with the company for expansion and improvement, 5) the social business is gender-sensitive and environmentally conscious, 6) the workforce gets market wage with better working conditions, and 7) the social business does it with joy.*

Social enterprise – *a business that prioritises impact over profit. It operates to cover its cost and aims to make profit, but ultimately impact comes before profit.*

Social entrepreneur – *someone who comes up with an innovative solution to solving a social problem.*

Social enterprises featured in this book

PlayMoolah: empowering the next generation to make smart money decisions with clarity and confidence (p.xxxi)
Mission: *Understanding the role of money for personal fulfilment & collective transformation.*
Activities: *tools, apps and face-to-face activities to help children and young people have a positive relationship with money, and use it to help them live their dreams.*
www.playmoolah.com

Toraja Melo: creating a market for the weavers of Toraja (p.53)
Mission: *to end the cycle of violence and poverty using weaving as an entry point.*
Activities: *creates fun and functional high-quality fashion lines and gift products made of Indonesian hand-woven textiles.*
www.torajamelo.com

Grameen Bank: banking for the poor (p.56)
Mission: *to offer credit to the poor to enable them to lift themselves out of poverty.*
Activities: *providing small loans (microcredit) to villagers in Bangladesh in a supportive environment that drives positive behaviour.*
www.grameen-info.net

SELCO: bringing electricity to the poor (p.57)
Mission: *enhance the quality of life of underserved households and livelihoods through sustainable energy solutions and services.*
Activities: *development, sale and maintenance of sustainable energy products and services to villages in India.*
www.selco-india.com

Empower Generation: women powering communities with clean energy (p.77)
Mission: *to seed and support women-led clean energy enterprises serving the poor.*
Activities: *training Nepali women to set up businesses that sell sustainable energy products to communities without energy, backed by microfinance.*
www.empowergeneration.org

The Fabric Social: jobs for women in conflict zones in Northeast India (p.78)
Mission: to lift the burden of poverty from women and their families in conflict and post conflict areas by economic empowerment.
Activities: creating high-quality fashion using textiles made by women in conflict and post-conflict zones in India.
www.thefabricsocial.com

Javara: preserving Indonesia's biodiversity and indigenous culture (p.80)
Mission: to keep alive Indonesia's heritage of biodiversity and indigenous wisdom about sustainable food.
Activities: creating premium food and drink products using ingredients raised by indigenous Indonesian artisan farmers.
www.javara.co.id

Krakakoa: changing the face of Indonesia's chocolate industry (p.82)
Mission: to improve the livelihoods of Indonesian cocoa farmers.
Activities: creating high-quality chocolate from bean to bar.
www.kakoachocolate.com

Color Silk: reviving weaving in Cambodia and ensuring livelihood for women in poverty (p.84)
Mission: to end the cycle of poverty for women in rural Cambodia by creating an ecosystem around weaving cultures and creating new markets for their products
Activities: provides training, raw materials and tools for weaving and gathers sales orders from corporates to ensure sustainable livelihood
http://colorsilkcommunity.wixsite.com/colorsilk-cambodia/color-silk-enterprise

Siam Organic: helping small scale Farmers out of poverty (p.86)
Mission: to help small scale farmers move up the value chain while making high quality superfoods available to consumers
Activities: providing non-GMO seeds to the farmers, training, field preparation, milling and storage, packing and distribution, business development and sales.
http://jasberry.net/

NOTES

1   United Nations. (2011, 12 11). *With Equal Rights, Empowerment, Women Can Be 'Agents of Change' for Sustained Socio-economic Development, Security around World, Third Committee Told.* Retrieved from United Nations: https://www.un.org/press/en/2011/gashc4009.doc.htm

2   An information economy is defined as one in which knowledge is the primary raw material and source of value. Web Finance Inc. (n.d.). *Information Economy.* Retrieved from Business Dictionary: http://www.businessdictionary.com/definition/information-economy.html

3   The Stanford Business Association of Stanford Entrepreneurial Students (BASES) Social Challenge is a student competition where students pitch business plans for social enterprises they plan to launch.

4   Economic Development and Review Committee of the OECD. (2016, October). *OECD Economic Surveys: Indonesia.* Retrieved from OECD.org: https://www.oecd.org/eco/surveys/indonesia-2016-OECD-economic-survey-overview-english.pdf

5   Groupon is a deal-of-the-day recommendation service.

6   UNESCO Institute for Statistics. (2013). *Adult and Youth Literacy: National, Regional and Global Trends, 1985-2015.* Retrieved from UIS Unesco: http://www.uis.unesco.org/Education/Documents/literacy-statistics-trends-1985-2015.pdf

7   UNESCO Institute for Statistics, *Adult and Youth Literacy: National, Regional and Global Trends, 1985-2015.*

8   Rosin, B. (2015, March 16). *What Start-ups Can Learn from Anemones and Boxer Crabs.* Retrieved from LinkedIn: https://www.linkedin.com/pulse/what-start-ups-can-learn-from-anemones-boxer-crabs-bob-rosin

9   Rao, L. (2011, January 6). *Confirmed: Skype Buys Mobile Video Startup Qik*. Retrieved from TechCrunch: https://techcrunch.com/2011/01/06/confirmed-skype-buys-mobile-video-startup-qik/

10 The framework conceives of eight forms of capital making up an 'ecosystemic economy'. Roland and Landua believe that we need to move beyond finance into living and cultural capital in order to adequately care for future generations. Source: Roland, E., & Landua, G. (2011, April). *8 Forms of Capital*. Retrieved from AppleSeed Permaculture: http://www.appleseedpermaculture.com/8-forms-of-capital/

11 Koh, H., Karamchandani, A., & Katz, R. (2012, April). *From Blueprint to Scale: The Case for Philanthropy in Impact Investment*. Retrieved from Acumen Fund: http://acumen.org/content/uploads/2013/03/From-Blueprint-to-Scale-Case-for-Philanthropy-in-Impact-Investing_Full-report.pdf

12 Hardoon, D. (2017). *An Economy for the 99%*. Oxford: Oxfam GB.

13 Ashoka. (n.d.). *Ashoka Venture and Fellowship*. Retrieved from Ashoka.org: https://www.ashoka.org/en/program/ashoka-venture-and-fellowship

14 Bornstein, D., & Davis, S. (2010). *Social Entrepreneurship: What Everyone Needs To Know*. New York: Oxford University Press, Inc.

15 YunusCentre.org. (2011). *Seven Principles of Social Business*. Retrieved from Yunus Centre: http://www.muhammadyunus.org/index.php/social-business/seven-principles

16 Rangan, V. K., Chase, L., & Karim, S. (2015, January-February). *The Truth About CSR*. Retrieved from Harvard Business Review: https://hbr.org/2015/01/the-truth-about-csr

17 Branson, R. (2011). *Screw Business As Usual*. London: Penguin Books Ltd.

18 Tonello, M. (2011, June 26). *The Business Case for Corporate Social Responsibility*. Retrieved from Harvard Law School Forum on Corporate Governance and Financial Regulation: https://corpgov.law.harvard.edu/2011/06/26/the-business-case-for-corporate-social-responsibility/

19 Veglio, F., & Fiedler, D. (2016, February). *Delivering on the Sustainable Development Goals: The Inclusive Business Approach*. Retrieved from WBCSD: http://www.wbcsdservers.org/web/wbcsdfiles/files/2016/03/WBCSD_Inclusive_Business_SDGs.pdf

20 Porter, M. E., & Kramer, M. R. (2011, Jan-Feb). *Creating Shared Value*. Retrieved from Harvard Business Review: https://hbr.org/2011/01/the-big-idea-creating-shared-value

21 Kim, J. (2015, October 29). *Ending Poverty: How Health and Innovation Can Lead the Way*. Retrieved from The World Bank: http://www.worldbank.org/en/news/speech/2015/10/29/ending-poverty-how-health-and-innovation-can-lead-the-way

22 The Guardian. (2005, May 15). *The Facts About World Poverty*. Retrieved from The Guardian: https://www.theguardian.com/politics/2005/may/15/uk.g81

23 Prahalad, C. K. (2006). *The Fortune at the Bottom of the Pyramid*. Wharton School Publishing.

24 Oxfam International. (n.d.). *Why the Majority of the World's Poor are Women*. Retrieved from Oxfam International: https://www.oxfam.org/en/even-it/why-majority-worlds-poor-are-women

25 Oxford Business Group. (2015). *The Report: Indonesia 2015*. London: Oxford Business Group.

26 Banerjee, A., & Duflo, E. (2011). *Poor Economics: A Radical Rethinking of the Way to Fight Global Poverty*. New York: PublicAffairs.

27 Banerjee & Duflo, *Poor Economics*.

28 Banerjee & Duflo, *Poor Economics, pp. 268-269*.

29 United Nations. (2015). *The Millenium Development Goals Report 2015*. New York: United Nations

30 United Nations, *The Millenium Development Goals Report 2015*.

31 BBC. (2005, February 3). *In Full: Mandela's Poverty Speech*. Retrieved from BBC News: http://news.bbc.co.uk/1/hi/uk_politics/4232603.stm

32 European Commission. (2016, June 8). *Deforestation: Forests and the Planet's Biodiversity are Disappearing*. Retrieved from European Commission : http://ec.europa.eu/environment/forests/deforestation.htm

33 Food and Agriculture Organization of the United Nations. (2010). *Global Forest Resources Assessment 2010*. Retrieved from FAO.org: http://www.fao.org/docrep/013/i1757e/i1757e.pdf

34 Merco Press. (2015, September 9). *A Forest Area Equivalent to South Africa Has Been Lost since 1990, says FAO*. Retrieved from Merco Press South Atlantic News Agency: http://en.mercopress.com/2015/09/09/a-forest-area-equivalent-to-south-africa-has-been-lost-since-1990-says-fao

35 European Commission. (2016, June 8). *Deforestation: Forests and the Planet's Biodiversity are Disappearing*. Retrieved from European Commission: http://ec.europa.eu/environment/forests/deforestation.htm

36 World Wide Fund for Nature. (2017). *Deforestation Overview*. Retrieved from World Wide Fund for Nature: https://www.worldwildlife.org/threats/deforestation

37 Food and Agriculture Organization of the United Nations, *Global Forest Resources Assessment 2010*.

38 Food and Agriculture Organization of the United Nations, *Global Forest Resources Assessment 2010*.

39 UNICEF. (2004). *The State of the World's Children 2005*. New York: UNICEF.

40 WHO. (2013, September). *Women's Health, Fact sheet N°334*. Retrieved from World Health Organization: http://www.who.int/mediacentre/factsheets/fs334/en/

41 UNESCO. (2015). *Education for All Global Monitoring Report*. Paris: United Nations Educational, Scientific and Cultural Organization.

42 UNESCO, *Education for All Global Monitoring Report*.

43 Girls Not Brides. (n.d). *What is the Impact?* Retrieved from Girls Not Brides: http://www.girlsnotbrides.org/about-child-marriage/

44 World Health Organization. (2014, September). *Media Centre: Adolescent Pregnancy.* Retrieved from World Health Organization: http://www.who.int/mediacentre/factsheets/fs364/en/

45 United Nations Children's Fund. (2014). *Ending Child Marriage: Progress and Prospects.* New York: UNICEF.

46 UNICEF Health and Nutrition Section & Liverpool School of Tropical Medicine. (2011). *Gender Influences on Child Survival, Health and Nutrition: A Narrative Review.* New York: UNICEF.

47 International Labour Organization. (2016). *Women at Work: Trends 2016.* Geneva: International Labour Office.

48 Elborgh-Woytek, K., Newiak, M., Kochhar, K., Fabrizio, S., Kpodar, K., Wingender, P., . . . Schwartz, G. (2013). *Women, Work, and the Economy: Macroeconomic Gains from Gender Equity.* International Monetary Fund. Retrieved from IMF: https://www.imf.org/external/pubs/ft/sdn/2013/sdn1310.pdf

49 UNICEF Health and Nutrition Section & Liverpool School of Tropical Medicine, *Gender Influences on Child Survival, Health and Nutrition: A Narrative Review.*

50 UNICEF Health and Nutrition Section & Liverpool School of Tropical Medicine, *Gender Influences on Child Survival, Health and Nutrition: A Narrative Review.*

51 Banerjee & Duflo, *Poor Economics.*

52 U.S. Global Development Lab. (n.d.). *Closing the Digital Gender Gap.* USAID. Retrieved from USAID: https://www.usaid.gov/sites/default/files/closing_the_digital_gender_gap.pdf

53 International Labour Organization. (2016). *Women at Work: Trends 2016.* Geneva: International Labour Office.

54 Yunus, M. (2005, September). *Grameen Bank At a Glance.* Retrieved from Grameen Bank: http://www.grameen-bank.net/grameen-bank-at-a-glance/

55 Barry, Z. (2015, April 16). *Now Is The Perfect Time To Be A Female Entrepreneur.* Retrieved from TechCrunch: https://techcrunch.com/2015/04/16/now-is-the-perfect-time-to-be-a-female-entrepreneur/

56 JMG Consulting, LLC & Wyckoff Consulting, LLC. (2013). *Venture Capital, Social Capital and the Funding of Women-led Businesses.* Washington DC: U.S. Small Business Administration's Office of Advocacy.

57 JMG Consulting, LLC & Wyckoff Consulting, LLC, *Venture Capital, Social Capital and the Funding of Women-led Businesses.*

58 International Finance Corporation. (2014). *Women-Owned SMEs: A Business Opportunity for Financial Institutions.* Washington D.C.: International Finance Corporation

59 Gates, B., & Gates, M. (2016, January 20). *Promises to Keep in 2016.* (B. Gates, & M. Gates, Editors) Retrieved from Project Syndicate: https://www.project-syndicate.org/commentary/gates-foundation-2016-priorities-by-bill-gates-and-melinda-gates-2016-01

60 Hande, H. (2012, March 23). *Affordable Solar Lighting for India's Poor*. (L. Rebecca, Interviewer).

61 The Mark News. (2015, June 29). *The Cycle of Dependency: When Helping Does More Harm Than Good*. Retrieved from The Mark News: http://www.themarknews.com/2015/06/29/the-cycle-of-dependency-when-helping-does-more-harm-than-good/

62 MittiCool. (2016). *About Us - Owner Profile*. Retrieved from Mitti Cool: https://mitticool.com/owner-profile/

63 The Indian Express. (2009, November 18). *The India of Ideas*. Retrieved from The Indian Express: http://archive.indianexpress.com/news/the-india-of-ideas/543155/

64 *Mitticool. (2015). Mitticool Home*. Retrieved from Mitticool: https://mitticool.com/

65 Mysmartprice. (2015). *Refrigerators Price List in India*. Retrieved from Mysmartprice: http://www.mysmartprice.com/appliance/pricelist/refrigerators-price-list-in-india.html

66 Fildes, J. (2009, July 23). *The Winds of Change for Africa*. Retrieved from BBC News: http://news.bbc.co.uk/2/hi/technology/8165262.stm

67 PRNewswire. (2009, October 2). *McGraw Hill, Publisher of Using Energy, the Book that Inspired Me Talks About Mary Atwater, Author and More*. Retrieved from The Boy Who Harnessed the Wind: http://williamkamkwamba.typepad.com/williamkamkwamba/

68 Yunus, M., & Weber, K. (2007). *Creating a World Without Poverty: Social Business and the Future of Capitalism*. New York: PublicAffairs.

69 Intel. (2016, June 26). *Mom Makes Smart Glove that Detects Epileptic Seizures*. Retrieved from IQ Intel: https://iq.intel.com/en-in/mom-makes-smart-glove-that-detects-epileptic-seizures-2/

70 Wall, M. (2016, September 27). *Counterfeit drugs: 'People are dying every day'*. Retrieved from BBC News: http://www.bbc.com/news/business-37470667

71 Yeebo, Y. (2015, July 31). *The African Startup Using Phones to Spot Counterfeit Drugs*. Retrieved from Bloomberg Business Week: https://www.bloomberg.com/news/features/2015-07-31/the-african-startup-using-phones-to-spot-counterfeit-drugs

72 Yeebo, Y., *The African Startup Using Phones to Spot Counterfeit Drugs*.

73 *Meaker, M. (2016, March 1). The Developing World Faces a Silent Killer. Could a $1 Solar Light Help?* Retrieved from The Guardian: https://www.theguardian.com/sustainable-business/2016/mar/01/silent-killer-kerosene-air-pollution-solar-liter-of-light-india-pakistan-philippines

74 Diaz, I. (2014). *Interview with Liter of Light Founder & Executive Director Illac Diaz*. (Z. Shahan, Interviewer)

75 Liter of Light. (2017). *Liter of Light - About Us*. Retrieved from Liter of Light: http://literoflight.org/about-us/

76 Diaz, I. (2014). *Interview with Liter of Light Founder & Executive Director Illac Diaz*. (Z. Shahan, Interviewer)

77   WHO. (2013, September). *Women's health, Fact sheet N°334*. Retrieved from World Health Organization: http://www.who.int/mediacentre/factsheets/fs334/en/

78   Branson, R. (2011). *Screw Business As Usual.* London: Penguin Books Ltd.

79   Ghalib, A., Hossain, F., & Arun, T. (2009). *Social Responsibility, Business Strategy and Development: The Case of Grameen-Danone Foods Limited.* Australasian Accounting, Business and Finance Journal.

80   Ghalib et al, *Social Responsibility, Business Strategy and Development: The Case of Grameen-Danone Foods Limited.*

81   Yunus & Weber, *Creating a World Without Poverty: Social Business and the Future of Capitalism.*

82   K, R. N. (2014, March 19). *Why There is No Fortune at the Bottom of the Pyramid.* (TEDxIMTDubai, Interviewer).

83   Johari, A. (2014, February 27). *Why India Has One NGO for Every 600 people – and the Number is Rising.* Retrieved from Scroll.In: https://scroll.in/article/657281/why-india-has-one-ngo-for-every-600-people-and-the-number-is-rising

84   Gettleman, *Meant to Keep Malaria Out, Mosquito Nets Are Used to Haul Fish In.*

85   Stanford, V. (2015, July 31). *Aid Dependency: The Damage of Donation.* Retrieved from This Week in Global Health : https://www.twigh.org/twigh-blog-archives/2015/7/31/aid-dependency-the-damage-of-donation

86   Stanford, *Aid Dependency: The Damage of Donation.*

87   Easterly, W. (2009, June). *Review of Dambisa Moyo's book: Dead Aid. London Review of Books (Unpublished).*

88   Frazer, G. (2008). *Used-Clothing Donations and Apparel Production in Africa. Economic Journal,* 1764-1784

89   Democracy Now. (2013, January 21). *Dr. Martin Luther King in 1967: "We as a Nation Must Undergo a Radical Revolution of Values".* Retrieved from: https://www.democracynow.org/2013/1/21/dr_martin_luther_king_in_1967.

90   OECD, The World Bank. (2014). *Making Innovation Policy Work: Learning from Experimentation.* OECD Publishing.

91   Yunus, Muhammad. (2005). *Grameen Bank at a Glance.* September. Retrieved from: http://www.grameen-bank.net/grameen-bank-at-a-glance/.

92   Aron, J.E., Olivier K., Laurent L., and Nowlan, A. (October 2009). *Access to Energy for the Base of the Pyramid.* Washington DC: Ashoka.

93   Goonj. n.d. *Founder's Profile.* Retrieved from: http://goonj.org/page_id=22834/.

94   Mortimer, Natalie. (2014, February 26). *"The Brands That Will Thrive in the Coming Years Are the Ones that Have a Purpose Beyond Profit" says Richard Branson.* Retrieved from: http://www.thedrum.com/news/2014/02/26/brands-will-thrive-coming-years-are-ones-have-purpose-beyond-profit-says-richard

95   The Guardian. (2005, May 15). *The Facts About World Poverty.* The Guardian. https://www.theguardian.com/politics/2005/may/15/uk.g81.

96   Spiegel Online. (2008, October 10) *Interview with Nobel Laureate Muhammad Yunus: "Capitalism Has Degenearated into a Casino".* Retrieved from: http://www.spiegel.de/

international/business/interview-with-nobel-laureate-muhammad-yunus-capitalism-has-degenerated-into-a-casino-a-583366.html.

97 Drayton, B. (2004). *Leading Social Entrepreneurs Changing the World (Activist Biographies)*. Ashoka Innovators For the Public.

98 Empower Generation. (2014). *Empower Generation*. Retrieved from Empower Generation: http://www.empowergeneration.org/

99 Empower Generation, *Empower Generation*

100 Diyalo Foundation. (2015). *Light Up Nepal: Diyalo Energy Program*. Retrieved from GlobalGiving Foundation, Inc.: https://www.globalgiving.org/pfil/21491/projdoc.pdf

101 Cherneff, A. (2014, November 19). *Empowering Women to Power the World*. (TEXxZurich, Interviewer)

102 WHO. (2016, February). *Household Air Pollution and Health*. Retrieved from WHO Media Centre: http://www.who.int/mediacentre/factsheets/fs292/en/

103 Empower Generation, *Empower Generation*

104 McAlpine, F. (2015, June 30). *After Years of Volunteer Work, This Entrepreneur Used Social Enterprise to Start Her Business - and Australians Love It*. Retrieved from Business Insider Australia: https://www.businessinsider.com.au/after-years-of-volunteer-work-this-entrepreneur-used-social-enterprise-to-start-her-business-and-australians-loves-it-2015-6/

105 The Fabric Social. (2015). *Annual Report in Brief*. Melbourne: The Fabric Social.

106 Mustopo, S. (2016). *The Story of Krakakoa*. (L. Hawkins, Interviewer)

107 Mustopo, *The Story of Krakakoa*

108 Mustopo, The Story of Krakakoa

109 Color Silk. (n.d.). *Color Silk Enterprise*. Retrieved from Color Silk: http://colorsilkcommunity.wixsite.com/colorsilk-cambodia/color-silk-enterprise

110 Color Silk, *Color Silk Enterprise*

111 Jasberry. (2017).*Our Story*. Retrieved April 25, 2017, from Jasberry: http://jasberry.net/about-us/our-story/

112 Jasberry, *Social Impact*.

113 Jasberry, *Social Impact*.

114 Wray, J. (2016, June 23). *Siam Organic Crowned Spark the Fire Pitch Competition Champion*. Retrieved from Global Entrepreneurship Network: http://startuphuddle.co/united-states/siam-organic-crowned-spark-fire-pitch-competition-champion

115 DBS-NUS Social Venture Challenge Asia. (2016, September 16). *Winners of the DBS-NUS Social Venture Challenge Asia 2016*. Retrieved from Winners of the DBS-NUS Social Venture Challenge Asia: http://socialventurechallenge.asia/winners-dbs-nus-social-venture-challenge-asia-2016/

116 Karnani, A. (2009). *The Bottom of the Pyramid Strategy for Reducing Poverty: A Failed Promise*. New York: United Nations Department of Economic and Social Affairs.

117 Sethia, A. (2015, May). *Marketing to the Bottom of the Pyramid*. Retrieved from Ideas Make Market: http://ideasmakemarket.com/2015/05/marketing-bottom-pyramid.html

118 Koh et al, *From Blueprint to Scale: The Case for Philanthropy in Impact Investment*.

119 Koh et al, *From Blueprint to Scale: The Case for Philanthropy in Impact Investment*.

120 Harvey Koh, N. H. (2014, April). *Beyond the Pioneer: Getting Inclusive Industries to Scale*. Retrieved from The Rockefeller Foundation: https://assets.rockefellerfoundation.org/app/uploads/20140508153451/Beyond-the-Pioneer-Report.pdf

121 Business Insider. (2016, September 8). *Hundreds Of Suicides In India Linked To Microfinance Organizations*. Retrieved from Business Insider: http://www.businessinsider.com/hundreds-of-suicides-in-india-linked-to-microfinance-organizations-2012-2?IR=T&r=US&IR=T

122 Business Insider, *Hundreds of Suicides in India Linked to Microfinance Organizations*.

123 Richardson, M., Bacon, N., Cochrane, D., & Tzigianni, D. (2015). *Social enterprise in the UK*. London: British Council.

124 Kinni, T. (2014, May 28). *The End of Work, Revisited*. Retrieved from Strategy + Business: https://www.strategy-business.com/blog/The-End-of-Work-Revisited

125 Budinich, V., & Drayton, B. (2010, February 2). *Get Ready To Be a Changemaker*. Retrieved from Harvard Business Review: https://hbr.org/2010/02/are-you-ready-to-be-a-changema

126 Koh et al, *From Blueprint to Scale: The Case for Philanthropy in Impact Investment*.

127 Koh et al, *From Blueprint to Scale: The Case for Philanthropy in Impact Investment*.

128 OECD. (2013). *Overseas Development Aid Tables & Charts*. Organisation for Economic Co-operation and Development (OECD).

129 Koh et al, *From Blueprint to Scale: The Case for Philanthropy in Impact Investment*.

130 Koh et al, *From Blueprint to Scale: The Case for Philanthropy in Impact Investment*.

131 Yunus & Weber, Creating a World Without Poverty, pp. 180-181

132 Koh et al, *From Blueprint to Scale: The Case for Philanthropy in Impact Investment*.

133 Koh et al, *From Blueprint to Scale: The Case for Philanthropy in Impact Investment*.

134 Koh et al, *From Blueprint to Scale: The Case for Philanthropy in Impact Investment*.

135 Koh et al, *From Blueprint to Scale: The Case for Philanthropy in Impact Investment*.

136 Koh et al, *From Blueprint to Scale: The Case for Philanthropy in Impact Investment*.

137 Mustopo, *The Story of Krakakoa*

138 Balch, O. (2015, June 24). *Beyond Organic: Promoting Indonesia's Indigenous Farming Cultures*. Retrieved from The Guardian: https://www.theguardian.com/sustainable-business/2015/jun/24/beyond-organic-promoting-indonesias-indigenous-farming-cultures

139 Kidder, R. M. (1989, June 1). *Every Tourist a Diplomat*. Retrieved from Christian Science Monitor: http://m.csmonitor.com/1989/0601/pten.html

140 Dear, J. (2010, February 2). *Howard Zinn: Small Acts Multiplied by Millions*. Retrieved from National Catholic Reporter: https://www.ncronline.org/blogs/road-peace/howard-zinn-small-acts-multiplied-millions

141 infoDev. (2013). *Crowdfunding's Potential for the Developing World*. Washington: World Bank.

FURTHER READING

To learn more about social enterprises, we recommend you read:

Bornstein, D. (2004). *How to Change the World: Social Entrepreneurs and the Power of New Ideas.* Oxford University Press.

Bornstein, D & Davis, S. (2010). *Social Entrepreneurship: What Everyone Needs to Know.* Oxford University Press.

Branson, R. (2011). *Screw Business as Usual.* New York: Portfolio/Penguin.

Yunus, M., & Weber, K. (2007). *Creating a World Without Poverty: Social Business and the Future of Capitalism.* New York: Public Affairs.

Yunus, M., & Weber, K. (. (2010). *Building Social Business: The New Kind of Capitalism that Serves Humanity's Most Pressing Needs.* New York: Public Affairs.

If you want to know more about the bottom of the pyramid penalty and the issues faced by the world's poorest people, we recommend you read:

Banerjee, A., & Duflo, E. (2011). *Poor Economics: A Radical Rethinking of the Way to Fight Global Poverty.* New York: Public Affairs.

BBC. (2004, May 19). *Shrimp Farms 'Harm Poor Nations'.* Retrieved from BBC: http://news.bbc.co.uk/1/hi/sci/tech/3728019.stmhtteting

Irwin, J. (2015, January 12). *Ethical Consumerism isn't Dead, It Just Needs Better Marketing.* Retrieved from Harvard Business Review: https://hbr.org/2015/01/ethical-consumerism-isnt-dead-it-just-needs-better-marketing

Lawrence, F. (2003, June 19). *Is it OK to Eat Tiger Prawns?* Retrieved from The Guardian: https://www.theguardian.com/news/2003/jun/19/food.fishing

If you would like to know more about the pioneer gap, we recommend you read:

Harvey Koh, A. K. (2012, April). *From Blueprint to Scale: The Case for Philanthropy in Impact Investing.* Retrieved from Acumen Fund: http://acumen.org/content/uploads/2013/03/From-Blueprint-to-Scale-Case-for-Philanthropy-in-Impact-Investing_Full-report.pdf

Harvey Koh, N. H. (2014, April). *Beyond the Pioneer: Getting Inclusive Industries to Scale.* Retrieved from The Rockefeller Foundation: https://assets.rockefellerfoundation.org/app/uploads/20140508153451/Beyond-the-Pioneer-Report.pdf

Sources of information about why women are better investments

Grameen Bank. (2005, September). *Grameen Bank at a Glance.* Retrieved from Grameen Bank: http://www.grameen-bank.net/grameen-bank-at-a-glance/

International Finance Corporation. (2014). *Women-owned SMEs: A Business Opportunity for Financial Institutions.* Retrieved from International Finance Corporation: http://www.gbaforwomen.org/download/women-owned-smes-a-business-opportunity-for-financial-institutions/

Katrin Elborgh-Woytek, M. N. (2013, September). *Women, Work, and the Economy: Macroeconomic Gains from Gender Equity.* Retrieved from

International Monetary Fund (IMF): https://www.imf.org/external/pubs/ft/sdn/2013/sdn1310.pdf

Klein, K. E. (2013, February 20). *Women Who Run Tech Startups Are Catching Up*. Retrieved from Stanford Law School: https://law.stanford.edu/press/women-who-run-tech-startups-are-catching-up/

Rubalcava, L., Teruel, G., & Thomas, D. (2009). Investments, Time Preferences, and Public Transfers Paid to Women. *Economic Development and Cultural Change*, 507-538. Retrieved from Duke University Scholars@Duke.

UNICEF. (2011, December). *Gender Influences on Child Survival, Health and Nutrition: A Narrative Review*. Retrieved from UNICEF: https://www.unicef.org/gender/files/Gender_Influences_on_Child_Survival_a_Narrative_review.pdf

USAID. (n.d.). *Closing the Digital Gender Gap*. Retrieved from USAID: https://www.usaid.gov/sites/default/files/closing_the_digital_gender_gap.pdf

ABOUT THE AUTHORS

Laina Raveendran Greene is the Founder of GETIT Inc., a strategic marketing consultancy based in Silicon Valley and co-founder of Angels of Impact (www.angelsofimpact.com), an impact network focussed on women social entrepreneurs helping to alleviate poverty. She is also Senior Adjunct Lecturer at the Strategy and Policy Department, NUS Business School; Associate Director of the Asia Centre for Social Entrepreneurship and Philanthropy; Goodwill Ambassador of UnLtd Indonesia; and, Advisory Board member of Acumen+Singapore. She has 25 years' experience in the telecom industry with a focus on Green ICT and bridging the digital divide in developing countries, and most recently worked in Indonesia where she helped raise several million dollars for a public-listed telecom tower company. An alumna of National University of Singapore, the Graduate Institute of International Studies in Geneva and Harvard University, Laina was one of the very first female techpreneurs in Singapore, when she started an e-learning company in 1997. Check her out at: https://www.linkedin.com/in/laina

Audrey Tan is the Co-Founder & CEO of Angels of Impact. Audrey's experience in technology began ten years ago with online commerce. As part of her stint in Silicon Valley, she rallied product marketing and business development for Qik.com, which was later acquired by Skype for USD$150M.

Audrey subsequently set up PlayMoolah, an award-winning social enterprise which educates children, parents and young adults about building a positive relationship with money. Audrey had the privilege of studying technology entrepreneurship at Stanford University as part of the NUS Overseas College Programme. She also published her thesis titled *Persuasive Technology and Games for Savings and Money Management* at NUS. Find out more about Audrey at: https://www.linkedin.com/in/audreytan

Lizzy Hawkins has spent her career working at the point where Government meets business. After studying history at Cambridge University, she managed government relations for the trade association for the British printing industry and then handled communications for an organisation which promoted British food around the world. She joined the British Civil Service in 2009 in the business department and since then has had a fascinating time working in a range of disciplines, from project managing the complex closure of eight large regional development bodies, to leading the commercial section at the British Embassy in Jakarta. Outside of work, she has volunteered for a number of charities working with homeless people and discovered her sporty side in a martial art called Savate, in which she proudly became the first ever British European Champion in 2007. Learn more about Lizzy at: https://www.linkedin.com/in/lizzyhawkins/

Printed in the United States
By Bookmasters